BEYOND GREEN

Why Should We Care About the Environment?

Dr. Steven L. Diehl

Beyond Green

ISBN 978-0-9883845-1-4

DD Publications, USA

****

The cover for *Beyond Green* was designed from an oil painting by the author described with the title, *Beyond to Higher Ground.*

Table of Contents

Thanks to my wife, Kristi, and her inspiring example of what it looks like to care about God's creation.

Thanks to our kids, who have embraced living sustainable lives with contagious care for the environment.

Thanks to the many people who encouraged this topic as being a relevant and crucial issue for the times in which we live. Thanks to the many friends who contributed thoughts and ideas.

Thanks to those who helped with editing, including my mother and father.

Most of all, thanks to the God of creation who displays His majesty every day in the world around us.

Introducing a Renewed Green

It is fashionable these days to talk about green jobs, green technologies, green energy, embracing green ideas to save the earth, "go green." What if some of these discussions are shadows and reflections of something that is much deeper, even more profound and real? Could there be mysteries and truth beneath the surface?

My wife and I launched out into a beautiful lake in our canoe recently, very early in the morning. It was a gorgeous day with a gentle mist over the water and a glassy surface ripe for slicing through. The reflections of the trees on the water provided a wonderful panorama to enjoy as we left a gentle wake behind us.

I learned something about reflections as we paddled across the water that day, something I had never noticed before. As we approached the reflections on the water, they seemed to move away from us. They were illusive. We tried paddling into them, consumed in the attempt to catch the reflections on the water with the front of the craft. It couldn't be done. Chasing the retreating images in front of our canoe didn't work, but the attempt actually advanced us closer to the source, to the shore beyond the reflections.

Reflections can be good or bad. Reflections of God's glory always take us to a superior shoreline. It is wise to pursue not just the reflections but the reality and truth beyond. There are deeper realities beneath the surface and truths more real on the shore of faith. There is a place beyond green.

This is a book about the idea of being truly green, embracing a healthy view rooted in truth. My growing conviction is that the highest motive for creation care and the purest description of what it means to be green is shared by those who believe in a Creator. Green is good, because it is about stewardship of God's creation. That is a shoreline which is real and worth moving toward with contagious enthusiasm.

Using our natural resources conservatively and restoring God's creation will not happen by accident. The currents of our day cause a drift further away, not closer to proper creation care and stewardship. Far too often, we become complacent in our lives and do not take action until we are either pushed to do so or row with intentionality in the right direction.

It was early in the morning when we took that canoe ride. I thought of a verse that has always fascinated me, "I will awaken the dawn" (Psalm 108:2). The idea of active participation in starting a new day is an exciting challenge. Why should we passively wait for the dawn to awaken us? Engaging life is more than sitting back and waiting for things to happen.

God invites us to walk forth in the works He prepared in advance for us to do (Eph. 2:10). This book is about the work of caring for creation, deliberately, intentionally, as worship of the One who made it all and holds it all together. I believe a new day is dawning with the advance of genuine green. Be encouraged to row the ship of your life toward a wonderful shoreline with a renewed green attitude.

I happen to be a follower of Jesus, so this book is written from a Christian point of view. If you are not a Christian, I encourage you to read the book with openness to that perspective and realize a shared commitment to caring for the world in which we live.

My conviction is that those who believe in a Creator should be on the front lines of what it means to be green, constantly pushing the envelope and spreading a grassroots movement of creation care. We do not have to wait for or depend upon government rules and regulations or pressures of various organizations to do what is right. Perhaps this book will inspire you to develop your own green theology in a way that inspires others.

My goal with this book is to awaken us to the opportunity for paving the way into new green territory, declaring the mystery and wonder of creation. My hope is to inspire followers of Christ to set the example for what it means to be good stewards of the marvelous world around us. We need to move further, forward, beyond green and into the realm of worship unto the One who created everything.

My hope is to inspire you to engage contemporary discussions of what it means to be honestly green and embrace a lifestyle which sets an example of creation care as opportunity for both worship and witness. I pray that this book inspires you to learn more about creation as a way to learn more about the Creator.

Some who share my faith in Jesus have said that biblical faith has little in common with the environmental cause. I say the environmental cause has biblical justification that is of profound significance. In this book, I will use the term *creation* with more frequency than *environment* as a way to honor the God in whom I believe and live for. I love God, and I want to love what He loves.

In all honesty, I have come to experience creation as a special means of grace, filled with lessons God has extended to me through a love for nature. Breathing deeply of fresh outdoor air and stopping to appreciate something God made is a way that I have tasted His goodness. Being alone with God under a tree with my Bible open is one way that I have found refuge and peace in Him. As the Bible says it, "Taste and see that the Lord is good, blessed is the man who takes refuge in him" (Psalm 34:8).

Love for the Creator's creation is a spiritual thing for me. I have experienced refuge in God on many occasions when on a mountainside or sitting next to a flowing stream. That is not meant to forsake the incredible value of fellowship with other people and active engagement in corporate church life, but to contribute to it. Nor does it mean that I have embraced some kind of mystical new age thought, even though I believe there is much wonder and mystery in the life of following Jesus. I am a solid evangelical Christian who happens to enjoy immensely the work of my Creator. If that is not your persuasion, I hope you can enjoy this book with appreciation for the view from my particular canoe.

A significant part of God's purpose in His creation is to reveal something of Himself to people. My hope is that this book will spark in you a deeper journey into the majesty of who He is. You may want to read devotionally, as much of the heart of this writing is built on the lessons God has taught me in the outdoors.

The world belongs to God, not us. My prayer is that God will use this book to awaken a deeper love for Him as the God of Creation. My desire is to help others love God by loving what He loves, both the people and the world He created for His glory. I hope that you are able to enter in, and that you are empowered to leave an inviting wake behind you for others to follow toward greener shorelines of faith.

Chapter 1

Greening Meaning

He makes me lie down in green pastures,
he leads me beside quiet waters, he restores my soul.
~Psalm 23:2-3a~

Green is one of my favorite colors, maybe because of Psalm 23 and the image of a peaceful nap in a green field. Perhaps I like green because it was the color of my BSA (Boy Scouts of America) cap, or that one of my USMC (United States Marine Corps) uniforms was called "greens," or because one of my first vehicles was a green Willy's Jeep that transported me and my friends to fun places. Green is a color connected with great memories. It is a color of spring pastures and summer forest paths that warm the heart with quiet, serene images.

To an avid golfer, the word "green" elicits memories of a soft, well groomed spot at the end of a fairway, surrounded by sand traps, where a great putt once brought a par score. For a financial person or someone who likes money, green is the color of their world. A woodworker would perhaps think of newly cut or unseasoned wood with the mention of the word green. An urbanite might think of a common area in the middle of the city where things grow and urban wildlife thrives. A nutritionist would agree that eating your greens is healthy.

In truth, green is much more than a color of the spectrum between blue and yellow. Green has taken on a powerful meaning of its own beyond being green with envy or having anything to do with an inexperienced rookie who is unripe or not mature. Green is not simply about the luck of the Irish, a color identifying decaying meat, or those recovering from sickness. It is more than the color of a gardener's thumb. A word which used to be rather simple in its various meanings has become complicated and in some cases charged with emotion and conviction.

Many things we don't think of as having any color at all are now green: power, food, tourism, cars, websites, and blogs. The green movement is not new, but popularity has risen to new heights. It identifies a common, complex, contemporary issue. We have green jobs, green technologies, and green energy. A wall in Baltimore is painted with the invitation, "Go Green, Buy Ethanol." Trash cans along the river trail in Harrisburg, Pennsylvania (called the green belt) are painted with the words, "Think Green."

It seems as though everywhere we look we see billboards or hear commercials boasting one of the latest green initiatives. I recently picked up a brochure in a restaurant printed to promote *JGreen Foods, Incorporated* (jgreenfoods.com). I received a card in the mail that had a "Green Tip of the Day" on the back. I purchased a shirt recently that bore the tag, "Eco Green---Wear Organic, Save Our Planet" (ecogreenco.com). I walked by a funeral home in Newport News, Virginia, which had a sign out front, "Green Award---by *Green Foundation* for landscaping that improved the beauty of the area." I thought about the contrast between the inside of a funeral home and the outside with its green award. Even in the face of death, green is alive. Green is in.

There is even a political party in the United States called the Green Party, with candidates on the ballot. Leaders of this party have created a document called "The Green New Deal," which includes a commitment to invest in green businesses, prioritize green research, and facilitate providing green jobs. You may not agree with all the politics and opinions of such a party, but you cannot deny the heart of their intentions to improve the environment and all the human systems connected to it.

How does God feel about all this? Is it possible that He is favorable toward certain brands of greenness? Does He like green? If He is the Creator, does He have a vested interest? I mean, the Bible declares that it all belongs to Him. "The heavens are yours, and yours also the earth; you founded the world and all that is in it" (Psalm 89:11). If He made it, He cares about it.

Green Beginnings

It would be wise to note that when we are first introduced to God in the Bible, we meet Him as a creative artist. He created green plants for food (Gen. 1:30) to provide for His creatures. Green in the Bible is often connected with eating, as the first book of the Bible indicates, "Everything that lives and moves will be food for you. Just as I gave you the green plants, I now give you everything" (Gen. 9:3).

Yet, the Bible's use of the word green goes beyond simply a color for fresh food. The psalmist paints a picture of new life using the warm shade of green, "They will still bear fruit in old age, they will stay fresh and green, proclaiming, "The Lord is upright; he is my Rock, and there is no wickedness in him" (Psalm 92:14-15). Green is a color of peace, tranquility, and quiet in the shepherd's Psalm, "He makes me lie down in green pastures, he leads me beside quiet waters, he restores my soul. He guides me in paths of righteousness for his name's sake" (Psalm 23:2-3a).

A group of hungry people actually experienced this beautiful image one day at the feet of Jesus as the Good Shepherd taught on a hillside. "Then Jesus directed them to have all the people sit down in groups on the green grass" (Mark 6:39). And He fed them.

Green in the Bible is also a color of righteous growth and strength. As the writer of the proverb said it, "Whoever trusts in his riches will fall, but the righteous will thrive like a green leaf" (Proverbs 11:28).   I think if I were coloring followers of Christ in a coloring book, the selection of a green shade of crayon would not be completely inappropriate.

What is Green?

We called it the *green machine*, that old Chevrolet Suburban that carried us on adventures all over the mountains of Montana. The thing just kept going, even though bad noises indicated it wasn't in the best of shape. It also earned the name "morphodite" for it's old age and longevity. I marvel at the sustaining power of the old vehicle, like it had good reason to live on, with purpose beyond its years. With all the places it took us, along with the challenges of getting there and all the memories built within it, the green machine seemed to take on a life of its own.

What does it look like to be onboard the green machine of environmental concern? What does it look like to be green?   Some people have chosen to live completely off the grid, detached from anything in society that might leave a footprint. They might categorize themselves as deep green. Others have rejected the notion of our ability to impact the earth significantly and have a cold attitude toward any kind of green movement. Some have capitalized on the potential for green technologies, while others have been put off by the emphasis and avoid the topic. There is a broad spectrum, from deep green to anti green and everything in between.

Some would say that being green means considering the impact of our actions on the planet, trying to leave the smallest evidence of our presence and the least significant effect regarding our use of resources. As a young boy scout growing up, I learned to leave a campsite better than I found it. We had a habit of poking a small green stick upright in the fire pit to symbolize an appropriately doused campfire. We always tried to erase footprints and evidence of our use of the area, so others could more fully enjoy the natural wonder of the site. With primitive camping, it often became a fun and challenging game to remove all evidence of our camp and try to discover where others had been. These were simple ways to express value for God's green earth to the benefit of other people.

Green is also a term used widely to describe buildings designed and constructed with minimal negative impact to the environment, highlighting conservation of resources and healthy, energy efficient spaces. Alleghany magazine published an article about a local man who constructed a totally green house.[1] Henry Maier and his wife, Nancy, built their dream home on Warrior Mountain, Maryland. They built it as an "ecologically friendly" dwelling equipped with solar panels and a private windmill, resulting in a January electric bill that was only four dollars. Whatever the root of their motivations in this regard, they certainly proved that it is possible to go beyond just talking about being green. Their hard work also benefited them economically, significantly reducing their utility bills.

For some people, to be green means more than environmental concern. More and more people seem to be combining both environmental and social justice issues. The argument is that the abusive consumption of one person can affect how well others are able to eat. For these concerned citizens, to be green in the simplest sense is to be aware of the need to care about the natural world around us and conserve the resources available to us in order to express our sensitivity to other people, both near and far. Poor agricultural practices in one area of the world can impact the ability of others to live a healthy life.   Economic factors and practices in one country can have an impact on people living in drought and food shortages in other places.

These are certainly valid concerns and the problems relating to the creation around us are worthy of our attention.   However, the solutions cannot be entrusted to global systems of control or left to big government regulations.   Helping care for our world will be found in grass roots motives and practices that are beyond politics and rooted in an appreciation for the Creator of the heavens and the earth. People like the Maiers made a personal decision to make a difference.   One person who chooses to live with a concern for creation and in sensitivity to other people can make a contagious impact, especially if it arises out of love for the Creator.

Embracing a life of fruitful creation care is a road to recaptured creativity that honors God. Revealing God's creative power through our lives and by our care for the creation around us can be powerful. It can be inspiring when others see in you a love for God through an appreciation for all that He created. It is never too late to make the difference that you might have made or be the influential person that you might have been.

Thawing the Ice

It isn't about a green machine, but the people onboard. There is often an unfortunate, cold tension between people who are passionate about environmental concern and those who are either apathetic or simply focused on other issues. There is too great a split between many Christians and many environmentalists who view each other with too much suspicion. The problems relating to the creation around us are real, and unfortunately divisive.

Christians, for example, have been accused of abusing the environment because of misapplied biblical justification arising from the command in Genesis to subdue the earth. We will address the real meaning of the Genesis account in a later chapter regarding stewardship, but the perception is a reality that must be considered.

However, it is unfair to blame poor care of creation on the Christian church. There are many other parts of the world with completely different belief systems who share the apathy problem as well as demonstrate downright carelessness with the environment. I've experienced the frustration myself when picking up garbage, wondering why anyone would flippantly throw their trash out the window without any regard for the impact.

For people who believe in God as Creator, there may be a combination of things that have caused the unfortunate reaction of apathy to the issues. Some have perceived that too much emphasis on environmental concern crosses the line into worship of *mother nature*. This has brought forth icy relationships with those who are concerned about the planet but may not have the same faith as a Jesus follower. People would do well to take down the cold stereotypical walls of "us" and "them."

One chilly morning last winter, my wife broke off some of the icicles around our house. Others were doing that as well, removing the danger of cold, sharp ice crashing down on people who might be standing unaware of the danger over their heads.

Sometimes we need to break the ice in relationships before that ice causes harm to someone standing nearby. Certainly you have experienced icy moments in relating to other people. It can happen with conversation about conservation and the environment. Sometimes it is manifested when a western beef eater shares a mealtime with a person who insists on a vegetarian diet. My conviction is that the only thing that can really break the ice is the warmth of love generated from the author of love and the Creator of all creation.

It is possible to have a misplaced sense of responsibility for either the planet or for the reputation of our Creator. Frankly, we sometimes simply have a need to be right. What keeps the ice hanging on is that cold sense of my rights, my needs, selfish motives and desires, icy I-see "me first."

When Jesus said that we should love our neighbors as we love ourselves (Matt. 22:39), the assumption is made that we don't have to work on love for self. Effort is required to accent love for neighbor. Love for self alone makes for a cold environment around us. Love for others generates warmth and life, perhaps best captured in the color of green.

Rather than reject groups of people who may be perceived as worshipers of creation and not the Creator, my passion is to build bridges.   Jesus built the most significant bridge of all, and said, "For God did not send his Son into the world to condemn the world, but to save the world through him" (John 3:17). God left amazing fingerprints in the world He created. Let's break the ice together and get to know Him better.

Vision for Swimming the Sea of Green

There are many people embracing the green movement, trying to live with renewed purpose in honorable concern for the planet. If you are a Christian with a creation interest, it could be that you are the instrument God wants to use for building relational bridges. People need to meet the God of the universe who created the world.   God may want to open your eyes to really see people who are searching for meaning in the world around them.

While at the pool for some aerobic swimming, I had one of those "God-moments." You know, those times when you feel like your eyes are opened and your vision is cleared to see something from God's perspective, an insight that teaches you something important.

My goggles became fogged as I swam. I started wearing goggles so I could swim more freely (not just to look cool like the Olympic swimmers). The eye coverings are very helpful.   I could see where I was just fine.   I could see the lines below me identifying the lanes for safe travel, but I couldn't see other people very well.   They looked cloudy.

Sometimes people deep into the green movement can be a bit illusive and foggy for a Christian seeking to understand the motives behind the passion.   That is also reciprocal.   Sometimes those who are passionate about the green movement can't see the perspective of people who do worship the Creator.

In the pool, I remedied the situation by washing out the inside lenses to remove the fog.   I thought of those verses in John 9:6-7, "Having said this, He (Jesus) spit on the ground, made some mud with the saliva, and put it on the man's eyes. 'Go,' He told him, 'wash in the pool of Siloam.'"   Siloam means sent.   The sent man went and washed as instructed, and he came home seeing.   I always wondered why Jesus used saliva.   Interestingly, saliva is used by snorkelers and divers to clean facemasks and goggles, preventing them from getting fogged over when diving in a cold lake or the ocean. I don't know why that works, but it does.

My vision is sometimes foggy when interacting with other people who might think far differently than I do, until living water from the hand of Jesus (John 4:10, 7:38) cleanses my heart lenses. His healing touch opens my eyes to see past my own position. His cleansing hand can help me see beyond the lane I'm in, past the mist that clouds my ability to relate to others more effectively.

I believe God wants to open our eyes and clear our vision from the inside out so that we can see people the way He sees them, even if they are swimming with a different stroke.

How did Jesus see people? He wept over Jerusalem and those lost like sheep without a shepherd (Luke 19:41). He wept in the face of those mourning death (Luke 11:45---known as the shortest verse in the Bible, brief but powerful). He repeatedly looked at the heart and embraced people where they were. He unfolded the goggles of a vision to make disciples by the touch of a God who cares. He continually embraced people where they were and taught repentance leading to faith which ushered them onto the path of life. This way is a new and living way, a brand new lane (John 14:6).

Too often I keep my eyes on the path that I'm on and I fail to take the time to clean the lenses which enable me to see others from God's perspective.

Some people around us are swimming deep in the green movement, and may seem to be in a different direction at the other end of the pool. Others may be antagonistic about being involved with environmental concern and we don't understand their inability to swim cooperatively.

Even in different lanes, we can swim in the same pool and keep away the ice. It is easy to focus on our own personal positions and swim along in our own way without looking for others to engage with grace. Living in creation care includes concern for those who live in the world, talking about the Creator and His creation in a contagious, winsome way. A.W. Tozer wrote, "Oh, how foolish can we get? The things that are closest to our hearts are the things we talk about, and if God is close to your heart, you will talk about Him!"

If God is important to us, what is important to Him is important to us. Creation was His idea and we are invited to see the world from His perspective through the lens of His Word. That includes opening our eyes to other people, even if they are different. That doesn't mean you should compromise good theology, but truth is to be proclaimed in love and not just protected with a walled-in defensive posture.

"A new commandment I give to you, that you love one another; as I have loved you, that you also love one another. By this all will know that you are My disciples, if you have love for one another" (John 13:34-35). May we all be ice breakers with other people who may have a different perspective on what it means to be green. May we clean the lenses and embrace renewed vision to swim freely and with God-inspired conviction in the sea of green.

Clear the Vision with Prayer

Certainly, some have climbed on board the green movement with the wrong motives. There are people aboard the green machine trying to steer in unproductive directions. They need prayer. People who worship the environment or *mother earth* are people who need the personal touch of the Creator. He is ultimately what the heart is longing for. The world needs people with vision, people who love God as their Creator, people who pray.

My old green suburban did not come equipped with windshield washers, so every once in awhile I would have to put the thing in park and wash the bugs off the window. It is easier these days with a window washer button on your wiper switch, but bugs are still a problem. The bugs (what's left of them) block the view and create a distraction. The bugs tempt me to focus on the windshield rather than where my eyes need to be——beyond the windshield to the view and journey ahead.

I've been inspired by a great book, *A Praying Life* by David Powlison. As he puts it, "In prayer, focusing on the conversation is like trying to drive while looking at the windshield instead of through it. It freezes us, making us unsure of where to go."[2]   Certainly there are bugs in the green movement. For sure, it's not comfortable for a Christian to be in the same vehicle with an atheist or a person who rejects the God of creation.   Yet, through Christ we can clean the windshield of prayer, get rid of the bugs, and focus on the God who creates and redeems. God wants the people around us to know Him.

With prayer as a window, we can have renewed vision for both the journey ahead and the people in our world searching for truth. That includes green truth expressed in love.

By the way, the created world around us is a front-seat window exhibit of the amazing creativity of the God of the universe. Creation is to be enjoyed and appreciated in a contagious way. To focus on the beauty of God through and beyond that window, rather than being limited by the less-than-perfect glass, is a practice that builds a more abundant life beyond green.

Love

Everything good is rooted in the amazing love of God. God is love (1 John 4:8, 16). To love God is to love what He loves. You can see it best in people who love God, but you can also see it in creation.

Have you ever studied symbiotic relationships in nature? There are lots of them. Some would claim that the driving force that encourages cooperative relationships between species of animals is the love of God. It is a mysterious thing, and doesn't always show up the way we might understand love, but there is something to it. There are the fascinating stories of birds and animals that mate for life, mating dances with attractional displays, and flocks that stick together. He is at work in and through all things. He is love.

We went with our kids to their church in Baltimore, called *The Gallery*. The worship team led us with a great blend of contemporary and traditional music. It was highly relational, diverse in ethnicity and age (the name fits), and the worship time was very biblical. The theme, expressed in one of the worship songs, was that we need to care for one another and carry each other in God's love. As the Bible puts it, "Carry each other's burdens, and in this way you will fulfill the law of Christ" (Gal. 6:2).

After church, we lounged under some trees by the harbor and enjoyed some peace and quiet together. As I reflected and chewed on the sermon I had just opened my heart and ears to, God gave me a visual aid. It was an answer to the question pounding around in my brain, "What does it look like to care for one another?" A pigeon was perched near us, bound up by fishing line wrapped around his legs. Somehow he had been in the wrong place at the wrong time and was stuck with a mess. Getting anywhere meant an awkward hobble or an embarrassing leap. Some people near us tried to catch him to untangle and set him free, but he would have none of it. He knew he was in bondage, but didn't trust those giants trying to help.

He did have a pigeon friend, however, who stayed near him. I'm sure that the other pigeon had limited expertise for removing that which was keeping him from freedom. Maybe in the process of being there with support, however, both pigeons could trust in the Creator together with the burden. Maybe that's what it looks like to care for one another —— proximity, coming alongside to encourage, being a friend, living incarnationally (like Jesus) with a peaceful presence that builds hope.

Maybe you are weighed down with something that holds you back. Maybe you know someone being limited by their belief system or lack thereof. It is easy to get wrapped up in displaced values and misunderstood love for nature that trumps worship of the Creator. It is also not uncommon to be bound by religious legalism that isolates you from other people.

By the way, one of the definitions of a pigeon is a person who is easily swindled or deceived (Encarta Dictionary). We all have a bit of pigeon in us, and we all get taken advantage of or even deceived. This is especially true if we are serious about loving and caring. Some of that has happened with misguided fringes of the green movement.

Maybe there is a strategic element to embracing a burden with someone else. Their burden may not be your problem, but it is keeping that friend consumed or even stuck. We may not know how to fix it, but we can always pray with others and look to the God of hope together. That shared burden might even happen out in the beauty of creation. It might help someone to see God's re-creative hope and stand a little taller. As it says on a plaque in a Virginia park, quoting Karle Wilson Baker, *Today I have grown taller from walking with trees.*

It hurts when people deceive us or speak deceptive words about us. It is a challenge of faith to open the heart to people again when you have been taken advantage of, scammed, or been misrepresented and misunderstood by others. It can be crippling, and emotional scars can too easily bring a limp that becomes a familiar part of us.

It isn't easy to trust again and walk with that joyful lightness in your step that God desires for you as part of the abundant life. Yet, God is a powerful Healer of the wounded heart.

To embrace the truth of God's incredible manifest love positions you to experience God as the lifter of your head. To live in His truth empowers you to love what God loves, including the world He created and the people He desires to set free.

Pigeons have a reputation of being able to find their way back home. Pigeons are also useful for carrying messages. Here is a message to share, from one pigeon who cares to another, words of truth that help us zero in on the depth of God's love:

> Dear friends, let us love one another, for love comes from God. Everyone who loves has been born of God and knows God. Whoever does not love does not know God, because God is love. This is how God showed his love among us: He sent his one and only Son into the world that we might live through him. This is love: not that we loved God, but that he loved us and sent his Son as an atoning sacrifice for our sins. Dear friends, since God so loved us, we also ought to love one another. No one has ever seen God; but if we love one another, God lives in us and his love is made complete in us (1 John 4:7-12).

Pigeons were born to fly, not limp around in this broken, fallen world. People are created to soar with love above the circumstances as worshipers of the God of creation. A wonderful relationship of true love was reality for the first humans in the original garden. It is that love God wants to restore with you.

There is a greening meaning. The understanding of green is growing and expanding in a way that has great potential to honor the God who created it all.

I invite you on a journey in the remainder of this book, a journey into the heart of God for people and His magnificent creation. Clear the lenses, thaw the ice, grow in love with the God of creation. Love the people He places around you, and sharpen your understanding of creation. Move beyond green, beyond the green machine with a life of its own, into greener pastures with a greater greener purpose.

"We are responsible because
we are response-able."
~Os Guinness~

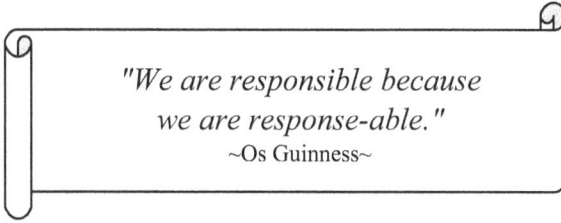

For Reflection/Discussion:

1. What does the term "green" mean to you?
2. How have you been influenced (good or bad) by the green movement, green technology, green initiatives, or green thinking?
3. What could you do personally to make a difference and increase your involvement in creation care?
4. Reflect on the above quote by Os Guinness.
5. Who in your world might benefit by a conversation about "breaking the ice?"
6. If you were asked to write a vision statement about Christian involvement in the green movement, what would it say?
7. Psalm 24:1 declares that the earth is the Lord's and everything in it. If it belongs to God, how might we better honor Him by the way we care for it and how we use resources?

Chapter 2

Tree Hugs and Harvest

The measure of a man's real character is what he would do if he knew he would never be found out.
~Thomas Macaulay~

Perhaps you have been in settings where lines are drawn in the sand and the environmental debate rages. One side paints people as "tree huggers" and the other side accuses "rape of the earth." There have been extreme examples of abuses on both sides of the issues. I have known friends in the lumber industry who suffered injuries from spikes pounded into trees marked for harvest. I have experienced the destruction of property by environmental activists who poured chemicals into logging and road building equipment.

I have also had friends who demonstrated very little regard for conservation, environmental concern, or the wise use of resources. I have known people who would rather fight environmentalists than consider the validity of some of their concerns.

Some animal rights groups have gone arguably too far, but others have done too little in the protection of wildlife and pets. I have known lumberjacks who were the most environmentally tuned in people I've met. I have also met people who fear having any association with any kind of green movement. There is certainly a wide spectrum on the matter.

Is it possible to be both a lover of trees, including all that is green, and believe in the value of careful stewardship with proper use of the earth's resources? Can there be a balanced perspective that honors God?

Certainly, you can discover in the history of Christianity some circles that made it possible to exploit nature in an attitude of indifference. Yet, there are many church leaders of the past who can be studied as positive examples. Saint Francis of Assisi was known to be quite reverential toward the created order. John Calvin wrote and spoke about partaking of the fruits of harvest, but that people must endeavor to be stewards under God in all things. Matthew Hale wrote about stewardship roles that should be intentional in protecting animals and preserving plant life, safeguarding the beauty and fruitfulness of the earth. John Wesley encouraged parents not to allow their children to cause needless harm to living things. The sum of their arguments might be articulated that man cannot claim an unqualified dominance over nature, but must embrace stewardship that honors the Creator of the world and everything in it.

It is time to recapture the idea of harvest in a mood of stewardship that honors God. Apathy is not an option, nor is deification of nature that puts the environment above the needs of humanity. There is a middle ground of tension between the consistent extremes.

Much of this has to do with personal and private attitudes, the choices we make regarding creation in our own lifestyle. How do you treat a dog you are not fond of when nobody is watching? Have you ever dropped trash on a trail when you knew no people were around? What resources have you used with disregard or ingratitude? These are issues of character; you might say green character. God provides, and He is honored by grateful treatment of His provisions.

Hugs and Harvest = Stewardship

In the book of Genesis, God gave an important command that invites us into participation with Him, "Be fruitful and increase in number; fill the earth and subdue it. Rule over the fish of the sea and the birds of the air and over every living creature that moves on the ground" (Gen. 1:28). What does it mean to subdue the earth and rule over it? Misunderstanding this passage could have terrible consequences for wildlife and the created environment in which we live.

What about the idea of "ruling" over creation? There must be proper understanding of Genesis 1:28. To "rule" is about proper, biblical, loving leadership more than domination and tramping down.

The New Testament gives great insights into what it means to "rule" and lead. Although talking about people, the implications can certainly be extended to creation care. Jesus taught proper leadership with the words, "For even the Son of Man did not come to be served, but to serve, and to give his life as a ransom for many" (Mark 10:45). Paul described the leadership of Jesus when he wrote, "Who, being in very nature God, did not consider equality with God something to be grasped, but made himself nothing, taking the very nature of a servant, being made in human likeness" (Phil. 2:6-7). The call of a Christ follower is to lead by serving. To lead people well is to serve them well. Ruling creation as a way to lead and serve other people looks very different than domination, destruction, and disrespect.

To understand the heart of it, consider the rest of the Genesis account. God gave every seed-bearing plant on the whole earth and every tree with fruit for food (Gen. 1:30). He also gave to the beasts of the earth and all the birds of the air and all the creatures on the ground. Everything that has the breath of life was given every green plant for food. That means God's care of creation was not expressed exclusively to mankind, even though humans are central to it.

God put people into the Garden of Eden to work it and take care of it (Gen. 2:15). This makes it an issue of stewardship and oversight. It means leadership and careful management. This is further explained and expanded in the New Testament. Consider this passage:

> Again, it will be like a man going on a journey, who called his servants and entrusted his property to them. To one he gave five talents of money, to another two talents, and to another one talent, each according to his ability. Then he went on his journey. The man who had received the five talents went at once and put his money to work and gained five more. So also, the one with the two talents gained two more. But the man who had received the one talent went off, dug a hole in the ground and hid his master's money.
>
> After a long time the master of those servants returned and settled accounts with them. The man who had received the five talents brought the other five. 'Master,' he said, 'you entrusted me with five talents. See, I have gained five more.'
>
> His master replied, 'Well done, good and faithful servant! You have been faithful with a few things; I will put you in charge of many things. Come and share your master's happiness!'
>
> The man with the two talents also came. 'Master,' he said, 'you entrusted me with two talents; see, I have gained two more.'

His master replied, 'Well done, good and faithful servant! You have been faithful with a few things; I will put you in charge of many things. Come and share your master's happiness!'

Then the man who had received the one talent came. 'Master,' he said, 'I knew that you are a hard man, harvesting where you have not sown and gathering where you have not scattered seed. So I was afraid and went out and hid your talent in the ground. See, here is what belongs to you.'

His master replied, 'You wicked, lazy servant! So you knew that I harvest where I have not sown and gather where I have not scattered seed? Well then, you should have put my money on deposit with the bankers, so that when I returned I would have received it back with interest.

Take the talent from him and give it to the one who has the ten talents. For everyone who has will be given more, and he will have an abundance. Whoever does not have, even what he has will be taken from him. And throw that worthless servant outside, into the darkness, where there will be weeping and gnashing of teeth.' (Matt. 25:14-30)

This is a parable about good management of the assets God gives to you and me. Blessings entrusted to His servants are to be faithfully stewarded and used for His glory.

An important question must be asked. What are the assets? Certainly it is people, strengths, talents, spiritual gifts, abilities and opportunities, but more. Is not creation itself an asset? Are not all the resources of the created order assets to manage properly? Certainly everything in the world around us should not be reduced to the banking of assets and deposits, but the principle remains. How we treat the created order is an issue of faithfulness. Hearing the words of Jesus, "Well done, good and faithful servant," applies to faithfulness that includes creation stewardship.

We are invited by God to take care of what He creates and provides, to care for what He gives us as empowered stewards. That means going over and above. It means more than just preserving. It involves caring in a way that lives out the idea of being "fruitful" as to the original command. Participation in making creation fruitful aligns us with God's provision of fruitful trees to enjoy.

All of this must include sensitivities to the people of creation.

Rather than hugging trees, why not people? Rather than harvesting in disregard for the needs of other people even in distant places, why not keep them in mind when using resources? That is stewardship where tree huggers and harvesters can find common ground.

Swimming Upstream

Embracing a renewed approach to stewardship and creation care will seem like swimming upstream. Getting serious about it is not easy. The green movement has grown into a strong current of thought and practice which is often flowing away from any connections to a Creator and sustainer of the universe. We must be involved in the green movement, even if it means going against a strong wave of opposition. Consider the words of Tony Campolo:

> Too often, when I read the books or listen to speeches of environmentalists who are not Christians, I recognize a basic shortcoming. Too frequently, they build their case for temperance and self control on enlightened self-interest. Adopting a more environmentally responsible life-style, they point out, is the only reasonable thing to do if we know what is good for us. But much more than that is needed. We, ourselves, have to become completely different people. An enlightened plea won't work. If we are ever going to change the world, our basic consciousness must be transformed and our essential selves converted.[3]

What we are addressing in this book goes beyond conversation. We may need to repent from our lack of involvement and recapture a love for God's creation. It also means a transformation of our values in terms of what "the good life" means in America with materialism and the motivations of profit. There must be a better way that honors God.

That better way might mean swimming upstream against the currents of our day. Sometimes the best direction for getting beyond green is to head upriver, but doing so in honor of God the Creator can be a source of tremendous joy.

Sitting on the bank of the upper Sacramento River one lazy Sunday afternoon, my wife and I spent some time relaxing. The joy in being together was enriched by the beautiful creation around us. We ate peanuts and threw the shells at each other for fun. We shared in laughter and reflection. We dreamed. There was a section of rapids in the river nearby, producing beautiful and inspiring background music. Kristi commented that she wanted to be that kind of Christian, bringing fresh water into the lives of others and never becoming a stagnant bug-producing pool of unmoving water.

The afternoon was topped off with watching a family of otters playing in the river. They are such fascinating animals. They provided a great image of a family having fun. They seemed playful with each other. Being curious explorers, I've heard that they rarely stay in one place for very long. Happy about the direction they were headed, swimming upstream didn't seem a challenge to them. Watching them was refreshing.

We thought of the words in the Bible, "Let the rivers clap their hands, let the mountains sing together for joy...." (Psalm 98:8). The otters were a song of joy. It was like they clapped their hands together as examples of God's creation singing of His glory.

Other critters also swim upstream in delightful ways. Consider the king salmon. This amazing fish faces overwhelming odds in fighting its way upriver, heading to the spawning grounds where it was hatched years before. This is a tough journey with many obstacles that can take as long as six months. They fight the currents with such focus on an end goal that they do not eat once they have entered the fresh water again. They have one purpose in view, to pass life on.

The female will lay up to 30,000 eggs, the male fertilizes them, and then the lady salmon covers them with sand and gravel. After fertilization, the parents drift downstream to die.[4] We can learn from the salmon, swimming upstream to pass it on. It's about life. It's about a joyful life like the otter. We otter have more playful fun at the river more often, even when swimming upstream.

Where Did We Get Off Track?

History reveals a downstream drift which threatens creation care and good stewardship. Part of it is simply, yet in a complex way, the advances in the industrial and technological ages. In the days of the Old Testament of the Bible, people sat around campfires and slept in tents on a regular basis. They drew water from wells every day. The weather had much more of an impact in their lives, and the rhythms of day and night set the schedules of life. Although many in the world still live in those realities, most of us in the West are removed and detached from such ways of life that keep people in tune with creation.

In addition, there have been various movements and ways of thought that have had significant impact. Gnosticism is one such line of misguided thinking. Gnostics embraced the idea that anything physical was evil and what was spiritual was good. This has contributed to the view that the physical world in creation is unhelpful for spiritual growth and nurture.

Then the Enlightenment of the eighteenth century, along with the scientific revolution, brought forth the scientific method. The thinking and practices "prodded, poked, and dissected nature, leaving in its wake a world no longer able to engender deep emotional responses of awe and wonder."[5] Science and intellectual advances promoted an attitude which enabled a detached approach, elevating people above the creation around them.

There has also been the influence of the more modern controversies created by fundamental issues of biblical truth and authority. In some cases, the distinction between general revelation (God revealing Himself in creation in a general way) and special revelation (God revealing Himself through the Bible) have at times left creation in a place of apathetic disregard. As David Henderson put it so well, "While their argument for the authority of the Scriptures was right, the evangelicals managed, as a result, to dismiss anew the tremendous value of nature in the life of faith."[6]

Perhaps there is wisdom in reevaluating the perceived need to focus on protecting truth and guarding orthodoxy at the risk of creation care. Yes, we are to guard our doctrine closely,[7] but good doctrine includes obedience to the first command of Genesis 1:28. The Bible does encourage Christians to be on guard and stand firm in the faith, but at the same time to do everything in love. "Be on your guard, stand firm in the faith; be men of courage, be strong. Do everything in love" (1 Cor. 16:13-14). It could be argued that proclaiming truth in love is more powerful than trying to guard and protect it.

Drifting into creation apathy because of rigid dogmatism does not honor God. Creation care and celebrating the God of creation is a great way to exemplify truth, live truth, and make truth known.

General revelation, as declared in Romans 1:20,[8] has profound potential to aim people toward the special revelation found in the wonderful truth of the Bible. People can meet God in nature (in a general way) and be inspired to further seek Him in the potent words of a book that is living and active in a mysterious and powerful way (Heb. 4:12). General revelation as discovered in nature cannot tell a person everything about God, but it can tell much. General revelation can help a person to get to know about God, but it takes special revelation to really get to know Him.

Getting back on track means that we can *hug* God by loving and caring for His creation as faithful stewards. At the same time, we can enjoy fruitful harvest of the wonderful resources He provides.

Resources of the Earth

Fracking….now there is a controversial topic. It is a word that spellchecker hasn't caught up with, and it represents a new and amazing technology. It is a striking example of human ingenuity and incredible engineering skill. It is one thing to dig a well straight down into the earth. The ability to drill a vertical shaft deep into the earth, turn and change directions, and drill horizontally nearly as far is something amazing. Accessing natural gas and oil in that way is advanced expertise, but full of controversy and debate.

Many are those who have fought for caution, even in honor of the Creator God, in the drilling for oil and the search for other resources. That is both warranted and necessary. Much remains unknown. How will it impact the water table in the future? What other problems might result from the invasive process? There are too many examples of abuse and misuse of man's ability to strip the land of resources. The fact that people are active in organizations to be a voice of concern is a good thing.

The good news is that many companies are investing wisely in research and the development of technologies that can have the least negative impact on the environment. Voices of encouragement in that direction are valuable.

It is good for people to know that the power of the One who created everything, even the provision of resources deep within the earth, is to be honored in the stewardship of those resources. Harvesting of resources cannot be disconnected from practices that facilitate honor and respect for the Creator. He laid the foundations and set the dimensions with some boundaries that need to be honored out of both respect for Him and cautious regard for future generations.

As the Bible writer said it, "May the glory of the Lord endure forever; may the Lord rejoice in his works — he who looks at the earth, and it trembles, who touches the mountains, and they smoke" (Psalm 104:31-32).

Or, as the writer of Job put it:

Where were you when I laid the earth's foundation? Tell me, if you understand. Who marked off its dimensions? Surely you know! Who stretched a measuring line across it? On what were its footings set, or who laid its cornerstone— while the morning stars sang together and all the angels shouted for joy? (Job 38:4-7).

Harvesting Winds

Global circulation is an incredible marvel. Because of the tilt of the earth on its axis, our world is unequally heated over the course of various seasons.   The inequalities cause temperature changes which drive the flow of water and air from place to place.   Circulations in the ocean and the atmosphere are vital provisions for life to be abundant on the earth.   Global circulations are the breath of life, with one provision being the wind.

You have to appreciate the perspective brought in Psalm 104, "He makes the clouds his chariot and rides on the wings of the wind. He makes winds his messengers, flames of fire his servants" (Psalm 104:3-4). The winds of creation are often *messengers* for me.

As I drove near Rawlins, Wyoming, I passed a ridge with over one hundred (I counted) very large and modern windmills. There they were, working hard in a dry and dusty desert with windy ridges, harvesting the wind. Wind is not always an enjoyable thing in a place like Wyoming, but the windmills were leveraging the negative wind and turning it into some positive energy. With extended arms, they caught the breeze in order to produce power.

The scene led me to reflection as I drove down the highway. How can I *turn* to position my life for God to use the storms? How might I leverage the circumstances so that the winds might not be wasted? It was one of those valuable creation lessons that caused reflection.

It led me to prayer, asking God to reveal the windmills of my spiritual life that will give me the wings for catching a harvest of blessings and extending hugs of ministry for His glory. It led me to think about those first disciples of Jesus who said something powerful when they combined a question and a statement, "Who is this? Even the wind and the waves obey him!" (Mark 4:41). Catch the wind to a life beyond green.

Harvesting Trees

I spent several years in the timber industry as a lumberjack in Montana. I love trees, especially western larch (tamarack) and fir trees. I also enjoyed the challenge of working as a sawyer. I still love the smell of diesel fuel or chainsaw gas mixed with sawdust on my clothing. It was the smell of hard work in the outdoors.

It would have been difficult for me to make much money as a logger because I always studied the trees and enjoyed them before starting the process of felling them. I also loved everything about a fresh stand of timber and how the forest might benefit from being thinned and logged.

Our practice in getting the trees out of the forest and readied for transport was to find anchor trees along the logging road to lean a pile of harvested timber against. Selecting a good anchor tree was always a very important component of a successful timber harvest.

I will always remember the day we piled too many logs against an anchor tree which was not able to hold the weight. With a loud crack, the anchor tree broke and we heard the unmistakable rumbling of rolling logs. The pile of logs tumbled down the mountain and damaged a few trees that we had wanted to save as seed trees. I was glad that we weren't below the pile at that moment. It was a valuable lesson in selecting the right anchor tree for the proper piling of harvested logs, anchoring resources rightly.

It is possible to love trees and be a harvester in a pure way that honors the Creator if you pick the right anchors. Try these words as an anchor, wise words about God as the one who is beautiful, strong enough to lean against, providing fruitful resources:

> I am like a green pine tree;
> your fruitfulness comes from me.
>> Who is wise? He will realize these things.
>> Who is discerning? He will understand them.
> The ways of the Lord are right;
>> the righteous walk in them,
>>> but the rebellious stumble in them.
>>> (Hosea 14:8a-9)

"The presence of God is the central fact of Christianity.
At the heart of the Christian message is God Himself
waiting for His redeemed children to push into
conscious awareness of His presence."   ~A.W. Tozer~

For Reflection/Discussion:

1. Reflect on the above quote by A.W. Tozer. If we are serious about creation care, how might that position us to become more aware of the majesty of His presence?
2. How have you experienced an increased awareness of God's presence in nature?
3. How is creation care a part of Christian mission?
4. How do you understand the distinction between general revelation and special revelation?
5. What are the challenges and obstacles to getting serious about stewardship of creation and becoming more "green?"
6. What resources are you in favor of harvesting that put you in an upstream against the current posture?
7. Reflect on Psalm 8. Pray the words to God.

*Either you decide to stay in the
shallow end of the pool or you go out in the ocean.*
~Christopher Reeve, Actor~

Chapter 3

Walking Beyond Green

For you make me glad by your deeds, O LORD;
I sing for joy at the works of your hands.
~Psalm 92:4~

Why do you recycle? I like to ask that question of people at the facility where we take our cans, bottles, plastics, and cardboard. I hear all kinds of responses. "To save planet earth," one man recently told me. Another said, "To conserve for the future and model something important to my kids." Some would say, "Because it's the right thing to do." The most profound response I've ever heard came from my wife, who said, "Because it's an act of worship."

Many of the answers to the why of environmental concern could be interpreted as man-centered. Our efforts fall short if the focus is on what we can do to save the planet, what we can do that would be the right thing, or what we can pass on to our children. Those reasons are good, but there is a more profound source of inspiration. There is a higher motive. It is being caught by a church I attended recently. Daybreak Church has several baskets in the foyer marked "Help Daybreak Go Green" with the encouragement to leave unwanted and used publications for recycling.

Walking beyond green is about worship. It is about worship of the Creator beyond creation. A trip to the recycling center is a healthy means of stewardship that demonstrates gratitude. Whenever I take a detour to pick up trash in my path because I care about creation, it is an act that honors God. Taking pleasure in watering a plant is appreciation for God's green earth. Letting the heart sing along with a bird enjoying an appealing back yard brings thankful pleasure to the soul. Walking in an attitude of creation care is a walk of worship.

Appreciating the Father's world takes us to higher places of declaring His worth. That is worship after all, living the proclamation that He is worthy. As A.W. Tozer said it, "Worship is the response of the inner man to the reality of who God is and what He has done." What He has done includes a creation that inspires a deliberate reaction of worship.

Worship isn't isolated to what takes place on a Sunday morning. It is a lifestyle of responding to the reality of who God is and what He has done, including in the world He created, every day. To take notice of nature's beauty and do something practical toward its care is to respond to the beauty of God's creative hand. To be thankful for the splendor of the earth He made is to live in reverential devotion.

My family consistently inspires me in this regard. They are always reaching over to pick up trash. My wife enjoys walking the roadside near our home to do some cleanup and improve the view for people driving by. Why does she do this? It is one way that she has learned to live in respect for the Creator. It is a striking and contagious thing. What a beautiful attitude to pass on to our children, helping them to see and appreciate God's fingerprints in creation and care enough to participate in keeping it beautiful.

Why are some Christians afraid of being involved in the green movement? Out of fear that accusations will put them in the camp of worshipers of counterfeits rather than the Creator God? Because it's just too much work and not worth the time? Could it be a distraction from more important things in the work of the kingdom? What I am suggesting is that we capture the heart of being green, not the politics or the economy of it. At the core of being truly green is a heart of worship.

As Webber puts it in his book, *Ancient-Future Worship*, worship involves proclaiming, enacting, and singing God's story as a narrative of the world from its beginning to end. Worship does God's story.[9] Christians would be wise to ask how they can "do God's story" through creation care. Worship remembers and celebrates God at work in the past, and lives in the expectation and anticipation of God's rule over all creation. It brings both the past and the future into the present so that people can actively engage in the redemptive plan of the Creator.

Consider the story as revealed in Psalm 104:

These all look to you
　to give them their food at the proper time.
When you give it to them,
　they gather it up;
When you open your hand,
　they are satisfied with good things.
When you hide your face,
　they are terrified;
When you take away their breath,
　they die and return to the dust.
When you send your Spirit,
　they are created, and
You renew the face of the earth.
(Ps. 104:27-30)

God gives living creatures food, controls life and death, and renews the face of the earth. Those who believe in Him worship Him and experience Him in greater ways by participating in loving care of His creation as a work of worship.

Fingerprints Sharpen Worship

My father-in-law spent years sharpening his gift of working with wood. He fashioned everything from oak toy boxes to cherry and maple coat trees, fancy hardwood lecterns, and practical benches built out of old barn boards. His woodshop contained all the tools he needed to create exceptional things. It brought him great joy to work with various kinds of lumber and build artistic creations.

The time, materials, and intense concentration required for his fine work of carpentry would not be fully grasped for those who have not endeavored to work with wood. It is hard work. It takes skill and patience. Nothing happens by accident, everything that happens is by skillful intentionality. It would be easy to miss, but the fingerprints and character of the hard working carpenter are sealed within the grain.

The human body itself reveals within it the character of intelligent design. Ask any doctor. We had a surgeon in one of our past churches who would often speak of the marvels of the human body.

The very fact that surgery can be performed on a human being is amazing. The cellular structures and the interconnectedness of body systems are full of lessons that lift our hearts to the praise of God as a masterful Creator.

I feel the same way about the created order around me. Have you gazed at a full moon lately? You know how it is, you look up at a night sky and marvel at the immensity of it all. You can't gaze at the stars or study the moon without wondering about the mystery of creative genius. As the writer of Psalm 19 put it, "The heavens declare the glory of God; the skies proclaim the work of His hands" (Psalm 19:1). Viewing the Grand Tetons opens the eyes to the remarkable certainty of a creative God. The more we experience the creation around us, the more profound are those first words in the Bible, "In the beginning God created the heavens and the earth" (Gen. 1:1). Every time I have the opportunity to be out in nature, I see the subtle evidence of God, fingerprints that stir a heart of grateful worship.

God is an artist of the highest order. He is marked by artistic, creative genius. Everything in creation reveals His artistic qualities. You don't have to look very far to realize this, and much of it reveals the smile and pleasure of the God of creation. Have you ever studied a bull moose? Have you ever been to a zoo? Perhaps you've praised God for a "great job" He did on a sunset? Have you observed the Grand Canyon, realizing that something happened there beyond the accidental? Can your eyes fathom the wings of a hummingbird? What about dolphins arching through the interface of sky and sea? Have you seen the courtship dance of a western grebe?

God is still creating and re-creating, and evidence can be detected everywhere by the observant eye. At a craft show, we spent some time in a crafter's booth that intrigued me. The vendor's display tent was filled with jewelry made out of fruit seeds. There were earrings made from cherry seeds and pistachio nuts, necklaces made from other various seeds, and even rings carved out of peach stones. One of the hosts of the tent was sitting in a chair sanding one of the peach seeds. It took a lot of work, but his labor was bringing forth the beauty hidden within the stone.

I was fascinated by the creativity of other craft people who were moving beyond recycling by bringing forth beauty out of what many would throw away. It was a source of worship for me to see the evidence of our Creator revealed with intentional release of hidden value. You have the potential for God-inspired creativity that reveals His presence and His work.

Creator Worship in the Word, Even in Winter

I experienced worship as I studied a leaf with a lesson while waiting on a park bench for my ride. Studying the shape of a leaf, I imagined robed hands raised toward the heavens in praise. I treasured the opportunity to redeem a season of waiting through a moment of worship. I thought about the words of the psalmist, "Let the heavens rejoice, let the earth be glad; let the sea resound, and all that is in it; Let the fields be jubilant, and everything in them. Then all the trees of the forest will sing for joy" (Psalm 96:11-12).

I also enjoyed a moment of worship while watching pelicans at the beach one day. They were diving headfirst into the ocean from great heights. I thought about how those amazing birds must have strong frames, and was reminded that God is my strength, my frame, my strong tower. I was inspired by the pelicans to dive more deeply into the vast ocean of worship unto the Creator.

Speaking of diving, there is nothing quite like the experience of scuba diving. Descending to the depths and seeing all the beauty is a rich experience. There is a whole world to be discovered beneath the surface of things. Diving, for me, is symbolic of going deeper into the heart of God, immersed in His colorful Word and His amazing world, enjoying the beautiful singing and silence of a deeper life beneath the surface. His Word is our scuba.[10]

Worship is about acknowledging the beauty and glory of God as displayed in His creation. To praise Him and enjoy His handiwork is worship. That includes other people of His creation. Creation is full of lessons and footprints that point us to the glory of God.

Even in the winter, when everything seems frozen and in hibernation, God reveals Himself. I have been through some winters that were all about snow. Snow is enjoyable. Snow is fun. Skiing, making snow angels, and sledding all make snow refreshing and fun. Something about snow shouts "Enjoy!" Making a snow milkshake with my family is a memory I find pleasure in. As the proverb says it, "Like the coolness of snow at harvest time is a trustworthy messenger to those who send him; he refreshes the spirit of his masters" (Prov. 25:13).

Snow is one of God's provisions for a thirsty world. In the mountains, snow is critical for providing a source of water to the valleys below. A good snow pack, melting slowly in the spring, is a crucial source of provision. Melting snow can soak into the ground to help bring forth life. When snow falls it has an impact—it can end a drought, and it will end up as water to nourish life. Like the Bible:

> As the rain and the snow come down from heaven, and do not return to it without watering the earth and making it bud and flourish, so that it yields seed for the sower and bread for the eater, so is my word that goes out from my mouth: It will not return to me empty, but will accomplish what I desire and achieve the purpose for which I sent it (Isaiah 55:10-11).

I like snow because of the purifying effect that it has. There is just something about a pure white blanket of snow that seems so spotless and fresh, like His pure love, covering a multitude of sins. Forgiven Christians are washed whiter than snow (Psalm 51:7; Isaiah 1:18). There is something clean and refreshing about this amazing thing called snow. Embracing a moment to enjoy nature, even during a frozen winter, is a mark of higher living. It is the purifying winter that facilitates a green summer. Likewise, pure motives stir a clean green movement that honors God.

We have a purpose, and it includes celebrating the presence of God in creation and letting that flow into creation care that declares His glory around us.   Contagious enjoyment is a big part of living a deeper and bigger green. God repeatedly expressed in the creation account, "It is good." He enjoyed what He created, and still does.

I can envision joy and even laughter in watching the water fall over stones and rush through gorges and gaps carved through rocky terrain. How could there not be joy in the sound of the birds or the rustling of the leaves? How could there not be delight in the sight of glimmering snow in the winter or the budding of new leaves in the spring? Enjoying the many wonders of creation is a way to bring honor and glory to the Creator of all.

Enjoy the Outdoors

In a moment of joy, I touched Kristi on her face gently. She responded, "That tickles." I was surprised and touched my own cheek in the same spot to test the effect, responding to her with, "Nuh-uh, it doesn't tickle." But she proceeded to inform me, "Silly, you can't tickle yourself." I had to stop and think about that.

It is true. I tried it. You can't tickle yourself. Go ahead and check.

God designed us in a way that we can't experience some things without others. In fact, there are many things we can't do without other people. Perhaps God is tickled that my awareness of that truth was heightened as a result of Kristi.

Could it be that the creation God surrounded us with is something He desires to tickle us with? Is creation care something that can help us share the delight of God with others? Perhaps we could lift the hearts of friends by telling the stories and lessons that God teaches us through nature. God may want to use you to help another person enjoy the beauty outside. "Be joyful always; pray continually; give thanks in all circumstances, for this is God's will for you in Christ Jesus" (1 Thess. 5:16-18).

It would certainly be appropriate to stand back, look at the sunset, and say with God, "It is good." See how many times He said that in the opening chapters of the Bible book of Genesis.

Confirmation of God's work is all around us, from winter snows to flowing rivers to the expanse of the ocean. We don't have to look very hard to discover evidence of creative handiwork that promotes worship and enjoyment of Him. It is often the simple things which help cultivate a grateful heart that moves us beyond mere environmentalism and into a devotional mindset.

I really enjoy camping, experiencing God's handiwork outside. So, why is it called out-of-doors or the great outdoors? The children of Israel camped after leaving Egypt (Ex. 13:20). They camped outdoors, out through the doors God had opened for them.

Doors are not supposed to be barriers designed to keep us locked inside, unless you are in prison. Jesus can go through locked doors (John 20:26). In fact, Jesus is the door to true, abundant life (John 10:1-18). To go out doors in Him is to enter in.

What does it look like for you to go out through a door God has opened for you today? What does it look like for God to BE the doorway for you?   Consider this passage:

> Therefore Jesus said again, 'I tell you the truth, I am the gate for the sheep. All who ever came before me were thieves and robbers, but the sheep did not listen to them. I am the gate; whoever enters through me will be saved. He will come in and go out, and find pasture. The thief comes only to steal and kill and destroy; I have come that they may have life, and have it to the full' (John 10:7-10).

Jesus is the door, the way in and out. As Jesus taught about Himself, "I am the way and the truth and the life. No one comes to the Father except through me" (John 14:6-7).

That's what camping outdoors has prompted me to be thinking about, the great news of out-doors. Walking beyond green might be a whole new doorway for you. Have a conversation with God about it. "Blessed is the man who listens to me, watching daily at my doors, waiting at my doorway" (Prov. 8:34).

Awaken a New Day

During a personal prayer time in the predawn hour, I was reminded of a fascinating verse in Psalm 108, "I will awaken the dawn" (Psalm 108:2). God empowers you to kick start the morning. As a follower of Christ, you don't need to sit back and wait for things to happen.   Jesus is the Light of the world, and He calls us to shine as stars in the universe (Phil. 2:15-16) as we hold forth the Word of life. We don't have to wait for the sun to come up if we walk in the truth that the Son has risen.

I'm not at my best in the early morning, but I'm glad God is. Many things in Scripture happened at daybreak.

At daybreak Jesus went to a solitary place to pray (Luke 4:42).

In Psalm 119:147, the writer talks of rising before dawn to cry for help and put his hope in the Word of God.

In Exodus 14, it was at daybreak that the water flowed back and covered the chariots and horsemen, leaving no Egyptian survivors.

A new day dawned with the conquering of enemies. The people of God were saved.

It was at the first light of dawn that the king got up and hurried to the lions' den to see if Daniel was alive, wondering if God had rescued him (Dan. 6:19-20).

It was at daybreak that Jacob received the touch that wrenched his hip after wrestling for the blessing of God (Gen. 32:25-26). At daybreak the people marched around the city of Jericho seven times (Josh. 6:15). At daybreak the Apostles went to the temple to teach the people (Acts 5:21).

Very early in the morning, at dawn (Matt. 28, Mark 16, Luke 24, John 20), the women discovered the empty tomb. It was early in the morning that Jesus stood on the shore and called out to the disciples after his resurrection (John 21). It was at dawn that the angels urged Lot to get himself and his family out of town before destruction came (Gen. 19).

Knowing that God's compassion is new every morning, flowing from His faithfulness (Lam. 3:22-23), what might be awaiting you in the morning? Be a part of a new awakening, a revitalized urge to be a part of creation care, as an act of worship. Get involved in the breaking of a new day of creation care that builds worship and witness to a broken world. God cares. So should we.

Creator Carpenter

I saw a bumper sticker once that said, "My boss is a Jewish Carpenter." The point the driver was accenting was that Jesus worked with wood, and still builds people who follow Him. He created us and He is the master craftsman, shaping and fashioning us as we submit to His hand. His creative hands are still selecting perfect tools to work on the raw material with which we were born. We are like blocks of quality wood with fascinating potential. I can look back on times of hammering and sanding, not understanding the pains at the time but thankful today for the results. He is still working on my rough edges, and I'm thankful that He knows what He is doing. The final product will be according to God's plans and for His pleasure and glory.

Following Jesus means being fashioned by divine processes. He is still a master at working in our lives, as we intentionally place ourselves in His woodshop at the altar of His workbench. Part of honoring His work in our lives is appreciating the world of His provision, His creation. He made it all. He holds it all together.

The creation story indicates that God created the heavens and the earth in five days, and then paused to find pleasure in the work of His hands. As it describes God's thoughts in Genesis 1:31, "God saw all that he had made, and it was very good." We would be wise to carve out the time to think in the same way. Stopping to appreciate creation as something good and worth stewarding is an act of appreciation to the master carpenter Creator.

One of the ways I have tried to express love and appreciation to my wood-working father-in-law is to show admiration and gratitude for his work. We have taken good care of the things he made as gifts for us. The lectern he gave us is a great work of carpentry, and we keep it groomed and polished. The bench he made us is given attention to keep it looking attractive. The transformation of raw materials into a unique, hand-crafted work of art is worthy of celebration and praise in careful appreciation. The labors of a carpenter often go unappreciated by the inattentive eye.

There are limitless opportunities to care for God's creation. To truly appreciate something means to care for it. Too often, we look at things like eating locally and organically, limiting our use of vehicles with poor gas mileage, reducing household waste, and searching for ways to use renewable, sustainable resources as trendy, liberal, and new-age. In reality, Christians should be leading the movement in all of these areas because to truly appreciate God's creation is to worship Him by taking care of what He has given us.

Being green, from the perspective of a believer in a Creator, means taking good care of all that God has made. It means His masterful work does not go unappreciated. We demonstrate our gratitude as we take care of His work. We declare His glory as we love what He loves around us. At the heart of it, taking care of God's creation, the environment, is an act of worship. That is something more than green, it is walking in appreciation for His handiwork.

Creation shouts of what God has done. So should we. "For since the creation of the world God's invisible qualities---his eternal power and divine nature---have been clearly seen, being understood from what has been made, so that people are without excuse" (Rom. 1:20).

May we find no excuses for failing to acknowledge God's beauty in nature. May we never miss an opportunity to worship Him. May we see His invisible qualities in the created order and thank Him. May we see His faithfulness in the rising of the sun every day and the changing of the seasons that display unity with diversity. May we hear His compassion in the songs of birds and creatures of every kind. May we walk in worship without excuse.

For you make me glad by your deeds, O LORD; I sing for joy at the works of your hands.
~Psalm 92:4~

Worship helps us find who we are and why God has placed us here on the earth. When we bow in God's presence with worship, only then are we made complete.

~Judson Cornwall~

For Reflection/Discussion:

1. Do you recycle? What is your motive?
2. How thankful are you for the way God made you?
3. What worshipful moments have you experienced when outside in God's creation?
4. Where are you in your spiritual journey? What comments in this chapter spark, for you, a deeper interest in Jesus?
5. What tool is God, the Master Carpenter, using in your life?
6. What Scripture has God used recently in your life to sharpen and purify you?
7. Where are you seeing God's fingerprints?

Chapter 4

Declaration of the Heavens

The heavens declare the glory of God;
the skies proclaim the work of his hands.
~Psalm 19:1~

Flying into Chicago, I watched an impressive thunderstorm from my window seat. The combination of a full moon, silhouetted clouds, stars beyond, and the dynamics of a nighttime storm were cause for a moment of awe. Over and over, huge flashes of light and long bolts of lightning invaded the darkness, strangely beautiful while fearfully powerful.

The perspective of a thunderstorm from above was amazing. I could easily envision written across the clouds, "Be still before the Lord, all mankind, because he has roused himself from his holy dwelling" (Zech. 2:13). Or, Psalm 46:10, "Be still , and know that I am God; I will be exalted among the nations, I will be exalted in the earth." Or, perhaps Psalm 19:1, "The heavens declare the glory of God, the skies proclaim the work of his hands."

It is fascinating how lightning works. The electric field of a thunderstorm produces "step leaders" to the earth. Objects (and even people) respond to the strong electric field by sending up positive streamers. When a step leader meets a streamer, strike one!

A lightening strike can kill you, but a warm beam of light from our merciful God is something marvelous to experience. That means He produces the "step leaders" and I respond with positive streamers. That is a pathway for flashes of light, riding on the positive streamers of praise in response to His lead.

The lightning reminded me that a stormy dark world needs repair and care. The time to be enlightened to this truth is more necessary than ever before, participating in the declaration of His glory as both beautiful and powerful. People who worship their Creator are like lights in the darkness with flashpoints of activity that make a difference, including by acts of creation care. Words of praise for the God of creation touch hearts with flashes of illumination that enlighten the understanding of the heart to the glory of God.

Glorious Origins

The story is told of Sir Isaac Newton making an intricate model of our solar system. A large golden ball at the center was surrounded by smaller spheres representing the planets, attached at the ends of rods cut to properly scaled lengths. It was built with careful assembly of cogs, belts, and gears that enabled the orbits of the planets around the sun to be exemplified. When a friend, one who didn't believe in the biblical account of creation, commented on the remarkable model, he asked Newton who made it. Newton was quoted as saying that nobody built it, that it just happened to come together by chance.

What a great message moving beyond science through scientific truth. A model like Newton's couldn't just "happen" any more than the real thing could simply fall together by chance into random existence. The Bible states it clearly, not in contradiction to good science, "In the beginning God created the heavens and the earth" (Gen. 1:1). The Bible also declares that only "fools say in their hearts, 'There is no God'" (Psalm 14:1). The skies proclaim that there is a Creator God, and the heavens declare His splendor.

In the sci-fi movie, *Contact*, Jodie Foster commented in response to the question of whether there is extraterrestrial life in the universe, "The universe is a pretty big place. It's bigger than anything anyone has ever dreamed of before. So, if it's just us, it seems like an awful waste of space." This was a key line threaded throughout the movie, first mentioned by her dad, repeated by her boyfriend who was a spiritual advisor, and brought to climax with her remark at the end.

In truth, nothing is of waste in God's economy. He knows just how to arrange, in an uncluttered fashion, His artwork to declare His amazing grandeur. The expanse of the universe is beyond measure, as is our God. The universe is bigger than anything anyone has ever dreamed of, revealing something profound about the Creator of the expanses. "Lift your eyes and look to the heavens: Who created all these?" Look up Isaiah 40:26 for a wonderful answer.

There are still stars, solar systems, and galaxies to be discovered. Some modern scientists have embraced what is called the M-Theory, which includes the idea that our universe is a massive membrane inside a much larger reality. Some of these theorists suggest that our entire universe---planets, stars, even architectural marvels like the Great Wall or the pyramids in Egypt---is just a "bubble" on an ocean of an existence covered and layered with many more like it.[11] Some would say this eliminates the need for God because it all arises from the natural laws of Physics. Others argue proof of a masterful magnificent Creator, pointing to the need for a supernatural finger which created the laws of Physics in the first place. At the very least, the expansive universe is a declaration of a creative grand reality beyond ourselves. There is more to what we see than what we see.

The Bible reveals a reality that is more real than what we can see, except through eyes of faith. It is declared in the heavens, and it has to do with worship. In Revelation 4, a glorious scene is described with Jesus as the centerpiece and voices declaring, "Holy, holy, holy is the Lord God Almighty, who was, and is, and is to come" (Rev. 4:8). At the center of the universe God is, and worship is happening around His throne. The heavens declare His glory and the ears of faith can hear the song, music that is real and close. He was and is the glorious origin, He is the wonderful God of presence in the present, and He will be forever in glory.

One of my favorite scenes in the movie, *Contact*, is when the lead character is attempting to transmit messages over the airwaves into space to reach her father. She believed he was "out there," somewhere. There is a Father who is more than "out there." The Bible contains a profound message that God is a Father who is near.

God the Father, the Creator of the expanses of the universe, is above it all and beyond what we could ever dream. At the same time, He is closer than we could ever imagine as the centerpiece of all creation. His glory is declared in the heavens and His work reveals His nearness. Although we may feel insignificant with the immensity of the universe, contact with God the Creator and Father is a reality within our reach. That truth brings a heavenly altitude that trumps our attitudes and moves us beyond.

Believers in a Creator God are getting a glimpse of the world from His perspective, gaining wisdom. Wisdom is the gift of His perspective. Wisdom expands our understanding in a way that can reveal glorious origins while taking us beyond our own green planet. As Thomas Mattingly II, Apollo 16 astronaut put it, "It's very hard to take yourself too seriously when you look at the world from outer space." From that perspective the earth is green.

Ten Powerful Words Declared

Did you know that the word *whodunit* is actually in the dictionary? According to the Encarta Dictionary, the word means "a novel, movie, or play centering on the solving of a crime, usually a murder." In other words, it means a detective story involving a mystery. Genesis 1:1 declares the mystery of the universe solved, not of a crime but of origins before crime existed. "In the beginning, God created the heavens and the earth" (Gen. 1:1). That is the greatest *whodunit* of all time.

Even scientists now tell us that time itself had a beginning. That means that the Creator of time must exist outside of it, just as is declared in these first words of the Bible. The Bible identifies a Creator who is God in the past, present, and future all at the same time. Jesus declared, "Before Abraham was, I am" (John 8:58). From the ancient times of the Old Testament, the Bible is specific in the definition of God as the I AM, outside of time and setting a created order in place before time began (1 Cor. 2:7).

In the beginning, God. This was (and is) a radical declaration of a Creator God who is eternally existent beyond time. Before everything, all of it, God was already God.

In the beginning, then, God created. We weren't there. No one was there, so we don't know the details of how exactly He accomplished it. However, we do know that He did it. It was said this way to Job, "Where were you when I laid the earth's foundation? Tell me, if you understand. Who marked off its dimensions? Surely you know! Who stretched a measuring line across it?" (Job 38:4-5).

Many scientists over the ages have agreed on this matter of God as the Creator. Even those who may not believe in a Creator God, supernatural design cannot be ignored. Stephen Hawking, one of the foremost contemporary theoretical physicists, was quoted as saying, "The odds against a universe like ours emerging out of something like the big bang are enormous."[12] Hawking goes on to speak about the ratio between the masses of protons and electrons as one of the many precise and critical numbers in the natural order. These specific and fine adjustments of numbers make the very development of life a possibility, pointing to divine design.

Another scientist, Fred Hoyle, calculated the likelihood that carbon would have precisely the required resonance by chance. He expressed his conclusions when he declared that his atheism was greatly shaken, adding, "A common sense interpretation of the facts suggests that a super intellect has monkeyed with physics."[13]

People who believe in God as the Creator of heaven and earth know there is much more to it than a *supernatural intellect* monkeying with the physics of it all. They have a foundation for understanding origins leading to purpose and meaning.

People who choose to reject that "in the beginning God created the heaven and the earth" experience life like a blind man in a dark room looking for a black panther. The blind person wouldn't look very hard for a black panther in the dark room. It would be preferable to ignore what cannot be seen. The tension of the unknowns would cause apathy at best. A little bit of light in a corner would be the best place to settle, with a focus on what can be seen. That does not mean, however, that the panther isn't there. God is not a panther, but He is there. Even better, He is the light.

An enlightened decision must be made at some point. Did humans create themselves? Did the universe just happen by chance? Or does the precise design of it all point to a transcendent, caring Creator? Which requires more faith to believe?

If God created it all, it is valuable. Anything emerging from the touch of a powerful holy God has great worth. If creation is more than just an explosion of energy and matter, there is value beyond what could ever be found by chance.

If the world around us is more than single-celled organisms morphing into incredibly complex life forms, what we see shouts of divine design. If "in the beginning God" means anything, it means that He is the center of all creation.

If God created, what He created is priceless and precious. What we do with this truth is the central value of being truly green. If we believe God created, then life has meaning. If God created, life has value and purpose. If we believe He is the master architect, then what we see is more profound than mindless chain reactions. If God created what we see, there is much more to life than respecting *mother earth*.

In the beginning, God was already there. In the beginning, God created. When these words of Genesis were penned, the earth was full of pantheism, polytheism, and idolatry. In light of that, the distinction of one God as the Creator was a sharp contrast to the prevailing thought of the day. The explanation of each of the creation days served to denounce the various gods worshiped in the ancient world, revealing that they were not gods at all. They were creations of men. Genesis chapter one declares that God alone is the maker of heaven and earth. God alone is the author of true green.

Cloudy Blue Skies

Sitting under a green shade tree one day, looking up at the sky, I was captivated by the remarkable contrast of color between the leaves and the deep blue color beyond. I thought of what the writer said in the Bible book of Second Chronicles, "He made the curtain of blue, purple and crimson yarn and fine linen, with cherubim worked into it" (2 Chron. 3:14).

Blue is one of the three primary colors of light. During Bible times, material was dyed blue for tabernacle tapestries, for hangings in the Temple, and for clothing worn by royalty and the rich. It can easily be embraced as a royal, rich color, like the heavens declaring the glory of God. The skies proclaim the marvelous work of His hands. The blue above shouts of the covering and the blessing of the almighty, royal, glorious Creator. "They are to take a blue cloth and cover the lampstand that is for light, together with its lamps, its wick trimmers and trays, and all its jars for the oil used to supply it" (Num. 4:9).

To walk beyond green is to enjoy creation under the canopy of His glory. Walking under a blue sky is enlightening, like a glorious curtain declaring the coming of spring. The blue sky provides a stage for the sun, whose warming rays will usher forth new, fresh life that we can care for and appreciate.

By the way, I've been told that a buzzard can be imprisoned by putting a short fence around it. The large bird has to get a running start in order to fly, so even a small fence can make it a captive.

People are not buzzards, but in regards to being able to find our wings we can relate. Looking up is the only escape from problems and temptations. Whatever fences keep us from flying, the answer is always to look up. To look up is to gain access to God's perspective. To look up is wisdom. Fixing the eyes upon Jesus, the author and perfecter of faith (Heb. 12:2), is the way to soar above the circumstances in a wide open sky.

Someone said it well with the words, "Sorrow looks back, worry looks around, faith looks up." Don't miss looking up to enjoy the blue sky and the sun which makes its circuit across it, where the glory of God is displayed!

Sunset Clouds

My wife and I had the thrill of watching an inspiring sunset once, at a place called "the end of the world" in Hawaii. It was a great place to rediscover the freshness of new beginnings with God. The sunset was the glory of God displayed. The sky is the place where great lights, the sun and moon and stars, display their radiance.

The big orange ball cast a wonderful path of reflected light across the surface of the ocean forming a long and inviting path to our observation point. It had the appearance of a well-lit passageway from the sun to us, orange light glimmering on the waters forming a perfect corridor across unknown seas. It nearly beckoned us to walk on the water toward the source of light, to follow the path by faith, to get out of the boat or off the safe shoreline and follow the light.

Following Jesus, Light of the world, sometimes means He will give us a path of informative direction ahead of time, like the angel telling Mary, "You will be with child and give birth to a Son, and you are to give Him the name Jesus" (Luke 1:31). Sometimes it means we won't know the details until after we've exhausted our resources of thought and effort, taking a simple step of forward faith. Joseph did that. He wanted to do what was right in saving face for Mary, and only then did he get direction from the angel who told him of the coming birth (Matt. 1:20).

Sometimes following Him might be an encounter with God in the immediate moment, like Paul on the Damascus road who was blinded by the light of the Son but had his spiritual eyes opened to walk by faith (Acts 9:1-22). That could be our experience during an encounter with God out in creation, walking the path of life beyond the walls of our often enclosed existence. For me, there is a growing desire to walk forth in what it means to appreciate, enjoy, and care for the creation upon which He shines. I want to not miss any opportunity to respond to the declaration of the heavens which usher forth sunrises on new days.

What about cloudy days? Even clouds can contribute to worship. Sometimes it is the clouds that accent a beautiful sunset or sunrise. It is the clouds that form artistic designs on the canvas of an expansive background of blue. It is clouds that swab meaningful colors in the sunrise of a new day. It is clouds that identify a layered atmosphere. It is clouds that provide the shading relief from an intense afternoon sun. Clouds provide refreshing rains. We live in cloudy days of confusing opinions, but there is beauty beyond.

Consider the rainbow in the context of clouds:

"I have set my rainbow in the clouds, and it will be the sign of the covenant between me and the earth. Whenever I bring clouds over the earth and the rainbow appears in the clouds, I will remember my covenant between me and you and all living creatures of every kind" (Gen. 9:13-15).

I find great encouragement in a rainbow as a reminder of God's promises. A rainbow is beautiful, but it also prompts an awareness of splendor in the midst of clouds and rain. Rainbows and sunsets or sunrises are packed with messages of colorful hope. Call me a mystic, but I believe in God's mysterious love for all of creation and the reminders He offers to the observant eye.

Cloudy Sunlit People Declared

The heavens declaring the glory of God often reminds me of worship in fellowship with other people. Sometimes, creation lessons and images prompt me to pray for people in the world around me. The big sky of Montana facilitated an incredible time of spontaneous prayer and worship on a drive across the flat plains east of the mountains. It was amazing what the sun was doing behind the clouds, or what the clouds were doing in light of the sun. People in my life came to mind as I observed the clouds. I prayed for them. My eyes were open with hands on the wheel, but more than my foot was on the accelerator as my heart advanced in prayer. With worship music playing through the stereo, it was a time full of gratitude.

The incredible colors on the edges of some clouds, like little rainbows encircling them, reminded me to pray for those for whom God might be adding color to the borders of their peripheral view. That included asking God to add a sense of "greenness" and raise up people to get excited about creation care, celebrating Him as the God of creation.

I asked God to gently shape people who are in cloudy trials and help them to become more colorful through the tough season they are in. A rainbow with intensity of color I had never observed before reminded me to pray for people who need encouragement through God's promises. After enjoying the sun shining through some distant rain, I prayed for those marked by tears clouding their eyes, asking God to shine colorful rainbows through their mist.

The sunshine breaking through misty weak spots and holes in a bank of clouds reminded me to pray for those who need the SON to shine in power through weakness. I ended up praying for myself as one of the people on that list.

As I enjoyed the landscape of the Rocky Mountains in the distance, I prayed for mountains and obstacles to be removed from behind the clouds of some friends. I prayed that they would have the kind of faith Jesus talked about, faith to move mountains (Matt. 17:20-21).

It was because of the clouds that I noticed the position of the sun. I prayed that the clouds of difficult circumstances would magnify the presence and position of the Son in the lives of people. I asked that God would open eyes to see Him even in the storms of life.

A cloud highlighted by upward rays of sunshine beaming to the heavens reminded me to pray with thanksgiving for the people coming forth as true worshipers. The rays of light emerging from the clouds looked like hands lifted to His glory.

Several layers of clouds, some shining as a backdrop, reminded me to pray with thanksgiving for those who do so much in the background behind the scenes. I remembered with gratitude the people who are serious about making a difference in the world, including taking care of creation in ways that might go unnoticed.

Some majestic clouds on the distant horizon reminded me to pray for those who may be far away, but whose influence on the shores of my life has been long-lasting.

I prayed with thanksgiving for my wife as I watched two clouds melt and mold into one (Gen. 2:24). I also expressed thanks for teamwork and unity in churches as a flock of geese flew in formation with a backdrop of distant thunderstorms. I prayed for those who are isolated and detached, as were some single clouds in my view.

Some transparent clouds made me thankful for people who are. The shape of an exclamation point reminded me to pray for those whose lives are accenting truth. A canon shape initiated words for intercessors who trigger the artillery of prayer.

I noticed many clouds which seemed to change quickly and dramatically, and I expressed thanks for the transformation that the Gospel of Jesus Christ brings to the lives of those who seek and follow Him.

I'm thankful for clouds today (both seen and unseen). They help me to pray in appreciation for the Creator and the protective atmosphere He gave us. The images created by unique shapes remind me to pray for friends and people who declare the glory of God by reflecting His light in a cloudy world.

Glorious Snow

Even what comes from the heavens declares the glory of God. Snow is a great example. Snow isn't just a covering, it reveals as it reflects. Sunlight on a fresh blanket of snow is a glorious scene to behold. Snow can be a mirror of the heavens declaring the glory of God.

Sunglasses are necessary apparel when the sun breaks out upon fresh snow. The glory of God is also something we cannot gaze upon in fullness. His glory is radiant beyond measure. It causes a pure, holy kind of fear. God's glory is spoken of in the Bible, in places like the Gospel writer Matthew, "His appearance was like lightning, and his clothes were white as snow. The guards were so afraid of him that they shook and became like dead men" (Matt. 28:3-4).

The prophet Daniel also used snow to portray the glory of God, "As I looked, thrones were set in place, and the Ancient of Days took his seat. His clothing was as white as snow..." (Dan. 7:9). The last book in the Bible also describes Jesus with an image of snow, "His head and hair were white like wool, as white as snow, and his eyes were like blazing fire" (Rev. 1:14-15).

I recall a morning of heavy snow when I shoveled my way to the front door of the church, and looked back at the straight path through a field of white. There was something unique and comforting walking a straight path to the church. It was an image of no distractions, just a cleared path surrounded by glorious snow. If the glory of God is my key goal in life, it keeps me on a clear path.

It is good to remember God's glory when we pray, "Thy kingdom come, Thy will be done" (Matt. 6:10). It is His kingdom, His will, His glory we desire. Snow, like the glory of God, comes only from above. "He says to the snow, 'Fall on the earth'...." (Job 37:6). God alone is above all, clothed in glory. We cannot add to His glory any more than we can cause the snow to go up. We can only identify, reflect, reveal, and point to His glory as we walk as kingdom people.

So, as the Bible proclaims it, "And whatever you do, whether in word or deed, do it all in the name of the Lord Jesus, giving thanks to God the Father through him" (Col. 3:17). Or, as written elsewhere, "So whether you eat or drink or whatever you do, do it all for the glory of God" (1 Cor. 10:31).

It is enjoyable to see people making the best of the snow. There is also something powerful about being around people who enjoy God's glory as they enjoy His creation. Creation shouts of His glory. The glory of God is seen in us when we are enjoying Him and His creation, including the satisfaction of creation care. When we take pleasure in God's creation, we experience His glory.

It becomes a matter of worship as witness. I like what a good friend wrote in an email in this regard:

> If nature is declaring God's glory, and we have been given dominion over nature, then we should take care of God's creation in order for Him to continue to receive glory from it, or to show respect for His glory by respecting this avenue of glorifying God. It is an act of worship on our part. We certainly don't want to

drop the ball here. And, the truth of nature proclaiming the works of His hands is actually quite a tool for sharing the gospel.[14]

The gospel is good news of God's creative plan. Creation reveals the presence of God and the truth that He created everything for His eternal glory. Snow reflects. So can you. Reflect His glory.

The Gospel in the Stars

Consider the constellations. Is it possible that God declared a message before it was warped by misguided reflections and distortons that show up in the astrology section of a newspaper? Could Virgo the Virgin serve as an arrow to the Virgin Mary? Might the Southern Cross reveal divine design in proclaiming the powerful work of Jesus in securing redemption? Could it be that Leo the Lion proclaims King Jesus as portrayed in the imaginative writings of C.S. Lewis? Could there be a message hidden even in the arrangement that might point to the good news Gospel message as told in the Bible? Is it too much of a stretch to point to the seven stars of the Pleades, seven being a pure biblical number, with even a consideration of the seven days of creation written about in Genesis?

It is dangerous to build theology or doctrine from the stars. It is unwise to seek to interpret messages from the heavens apart from biblical truth. Astrology and other cultish systems are counterfeit imitations which can contain just enough truth and believability to become distractions.

Yet, the Bible affirms God's hand in nature. It makes sense to see some level of general revelation in the stars. The verse is worth repeating, penned by Paul, "For since the creation of the world God's invisible qualities — his eternal power and divine nature — have been clearly seen, being understood from what has been made, so that men are without excuse" (Rom. 1:20).

The heavens do declare His glory. Maybe it is possible to see glimpses of God's design and insights into His heart even in the patterns of the heavens. As the Old Testament book of Job says, ""Can you bind the beautiful Pleiades? Can you loose the cords of Orion? Can you bring forth the constellations in their seasons or lead out the Bear with its cubs? Do you know the laws of the heavens? Can you set up [God's] dominion over the earth?" (Job 38:31-33).

The constellations and their stars are amazing when you view them in remote areas where no city lights can hinder the God-made brilliance. In the farm country of Iowa, at a recent family reunion, we got a taste of the bright starlit panorama accented by dark sky and highlighted by fireflies all around us. I remembered the words of the Bible, "He determines the number of the stars and calls them each by name. Great is our Lord and mighty in power; his understanding has no limit" (Psalm 147:4-5).

One of my favorite places in the world is along the Musselshell River in Montana, where it joins the Missouri River. It is an amazing place. I recall camping there one night, the nearest ranch nearly twenty miles away, no man-made lights to hinder the stars above. The darkness of the sky magnified the illuminating stars of the heavens without the distracting disruption of unnatural lights.

Many false, man-made lights distract the eyes of people from seeing the majesty of God, including false religions and even self-righteous practices and attitudes which cultivate legalistic spiritual pride with its false promises. As Kepler said it, it is the glory of God and not the glory of our own minds, no matter how smart we think we are. "The god of this age has blinded the minds of unbelievers, so that they cannot see the light of the gospel of the glory of Christ, who is the image of God" (2 Cor. 4:5).

The constellations are one amazing aspect of the heavens, but did you also know that the Bible compares people to stars? "Do everything without complaining or arguing, so that you may become blameless and pure, children of God without fault in a crooked and depraved generation, in which you shine like stars in the universe as you hold out the word of life...." (Phil. 2:14-16a). Perhaps the next time you admire the stars you can remember that following Jesus and holding onto His word of life empowers an attractive shine.

I am reading a book about solitude as a spiritual discipline, and I am reminded of how refreshing it is to get away and be alone with Jesus, Light of the world, who is building a kingdom of light(s). Time alone with God strengthens our shine.

The stars are brighter when the sky is darker. The stronger the darkness, the more pronounced His glorious light. As we live in this dark, "crooked and depraved" world (Phil. 2:15), we are invited to shine. It is good to enjoy and appreciate the heavens as they declare the glory of God. When darkness closes in and false light distracts, you can shine by plugging into a brighter life of truth that lifts you above the circumstances.

Did you know that Venus, relative to other planets, spins backward on its axis? The evening star spins the opposite direction and is the brightest light in the evening sky. Celebrating a Creator of creation may seem counter to the movement of many in our world, but it is a beautiful way to shine.

Johann Kepler (1571 – 1630) is considered to be the founder of physical astronomy. Did you also know that he studied for two years in a seminary? Kepler wrote in one of his books, "Since we astronomers are priests of the highest God in regard to the book of nature, it befits us to be thoughtful, not of the glory of our minds, but rather, above all else, of the glory of God."[15]

The Glory of Light

The first thing God spoke into existence was light (Gen. 1:3). Light is amazing. The spectrum reveals rainbow colors as the fingerprints of a creative God. That eternal place called heaven will be marked by the absence of dark nights and the presence of glorious light. As the writer declares it, "There will be no more night. They will not need the light of a lamp or the light of the sun, for the Lord God will give them light. And they will reign for ever and ever" (Rev. 22:5).

There are tastes of that in creation. Consider the arctic tern who lives in nearly eight months of continual daylight by migrating from one pole to the other. The tern reminds me of a Bible verse that turns my heart toward praise, "In the heavens he has pitched a tent for the sun, which is like a bridegroom coming forth from his pavilion, like a champion rejoicing to run his course" (Psalm 19:4-5). The sun generates light in an amazing way to sustain life on earth.

The moon is 238,850 miles away. That is close in space terms, and even with it's proximity it is very different than the earth. Did you know that it is slowly spiraling away from us? When we look at the moon, we always see the same side because of what is known as "synchronous rotation." That means that the Moon turns on its axis in exactly the same time (27.3 days) that it takes to orbit the earth. That kind of physics shouts of a divine Creator.

In that place called heaven, the sun and moon will be insignificant in light of their Creator. As the final Bible book declares, "The city does not need the sun or the moon to shine on it, for the glory of God gives it light, and the Lamb is its lamp" (Rev. 21:23).

The moon reflects the light of the sun. Likewise, you can reflect Jesus. "And we, who with unveiled faces all reflect the Lord's glory, are being transformed into his likeness with ever-increasing glory, which comes from the Lord, who is the Spirit" (2 Cor. 3:18). The next time you see the sunset and enjoy the moon, let your pleasure and appreciation be reflected to others around you as an act of worship. That will declare the glory of God. That is deep green.

The invitation to followers of Jesus is to be light in the darkness (Matt. 5:14-16). Part of that means loving light and sharing light even in the world of creation care and green involvement. A proper understanding of creation care means Christian mission even to the point of Christian vocation. It is honorable to take on a job or even become an entrepreneur in green technologies that bring light to the field. That is a merging of mission and vocation that honors the Creator and inspires others to care.

If the world is truly going to hear the message of creation care, it will be most effectively accomplished through a united body of people. God's body of people represents the visible manifestation of Jesus on earth, the Christian church, the collection of Jesus followers who live in the light of the glorious Creator.

Smoke and Smokescreens

Bad, smoky fires are not unusual out west. They become a part of life. I recall stepping outside one morning to the overwhelming smell of smoke. I had to suppress a cough. The visibility was very poor. One of the challenges on those kinds of western days is that new fires can be hidden in the smoke of existing fires, making it difficult for firefighters to spot new flames. In a bad fire season, the smaller fires can do great damage before they are discovered.

There are many little fires in the green movement, hidden in the smoke of even larger threats. Sometimes there are aspects of the green movement that can distort and cover the light of true creation concern and even hinder or hide the declaration of God's glory. You don't have to search very hard on the internet to discover distorted views of the environment and nature. People can easily be deceived by cultural smoke that hides those smaller but dangerous new fires.

As the prophet wrote, "Surely wickedness burns like a fire; it consumes briers and thorns, it sets the forest thickets ablaze, so that it rolls upward in a column of smoke" (Isaiah 9:18). Worship of nature could be identified as something wicked. That sounds harsh, but that is the way the Bible puts it. Worship of creation rather than the Creator is wicked because it puts out the flame on the wick of reverence and respect for the God of all creation. God alone is worthy of our worship.

Worship of nature is not new. The Old Testament is full of examples of idol worship, people bowing down to the many gods of nature. Consider the Old Testament story of Ahaz. "And he sacrificed and made offerings on the high places and on the hills and under every green tree" (2 Chron. 28:4). Ahaz, when he became king at twenty years old, "did not do what was right in the eyes of the Lord." He encouraged metal images of the Baals.

Some days the horizon seems fogged over with problems, like a smoky western morning. Sometimes the struggles people are facing (or causing) bring cloudy skies. God's glory is not at threat. God's glory is not out of sight. No smoke can stop the declaration of His glory, and sometimes it is the smoke that creates colorful mornings because of the sun beyond.

Creation Song

Praying on the back porch one beautiful morning, the tune of a songbird caught our ears. Other birds began to sing, contributing harmony. It was a God-moment that brought a wonderful hush to our spirits. It wasn't quiet, but our hearts were silenced. We couldn't see the source of the melodic creation songs, but we experienced the pleasure of a mysterious moment.

In harmonic solitude of that kind, the heart can tune in to God as the Author of all the created order. I reflected on the words of the prophet, "The Lord is in his holy temple. Let all the earth keep silence before him" (Hab. 2:20). Or the words of King Solomon when he prayed, "The heavens, even the highest heaven, cannot contain you. How much less this temple I have built!" (1 Kings 8:27). This is wonderful music, God's music, declarations of the heavens to His glory.

I'm listening for that silent song with more deliberation since that morning. My appreciation of the created world outside grows through experiences like that. I like the way David Henderson said it, "Stepping out of the right-angled world of interiors into God's variegated realm of curves and colors brings a fresh readiness to hear the voice of the One who made us."[16] Intentional contact with God's handiwork in creation sparks a profound sense of His presence and His voice.

Jesus posed a question one day as He walked in creation. I'd like to believe that He pointed to a tree as He spoke. "What is the kingdom of God like? What shall I compare it to? It is like a mustard seed, which a man took and planted in his garden. It grew and became a tree, and the birds of the air perched in its branches" (Luke 13:18-19).

The birds seem to declare a peaceful kingdom song, like the heavens declaring the glory of God, the skies proclaiming the work of His hands, their voice going out into all the earth (Psalm 19:1-4). The birds sing small, pleasant songs, recognizable but not overwhelming or overbearing. The mustard seed was the smallest known seed to the audience of Jesus when He spoke the words of Luke 13:18-19. However, A tiny mustard seed produces the mustard tree, a large herbal plant that grows to be eight to twelve feet tall.

The tree is a place where birds make their nests. It is a place of refuge and protection. When God takes a small faith and produces something big, it can provide peace, refuge, and a sense of hope for others. A small seed producing a tree is a powerful illustration of supernatural results from the smallest faith. A tree which has grown supernaturally provides a safe haven, a place where songs can be sung. It's a kingdom song, with a rising pitch and increasing tempo.

Supernatural results are produced when we tune in to God's song, even with undersized expressions of faith when we don't feel like making music. It's a song of a growing kingdom. It is a song sung when good stewardship and creation care are manifested. Tune in and sing. Join with the birds, along with all of creation, to declare the glory of God and bear witness to the marvelous work of His hands. That is life beyond green.

> *The natural world bears the signature of a supernatural Creator.*
>
> ~Henry G. Bosch~

For Reflection/Discussion:

1. What is your favorite star, constellation, or planet? How does it point to God's glory?
2. If you could get a glimpse of your current situation from the viewpoint of outer space, what might change?
3. What changes might occur for a person who begins to believe that God, in the beginning, created the heavens and the earth?
4. When we pray the prayer, "Thy kingdom come, Thy will be done," how might that include restoring beauty in creation?
5. Where do you need God's light to shine? What darkness is in your world? Read Matthew 5:14-16 and talk about it.
6. Reflect on the last time a songbird or the sound of an insect caught your ear. In what way might that have been a *stop sign moment* giving you opportunity to worship the God of creation?
7. What are some of the distractions that prevent people from believing in God as their Creator?

Chapter 5

Green Voices of the Earth

Their voice goes out into all the earth, their words
to the ends of the world.
~Psalm 19:4a~

I can't imagine a book greener than the Bible. I mean, what is your favorite realm of the environment? Are you attracted to water settings? Read in the Bible the numerous stories about the Red Sea, the Jordan River, the Nile, the Sea of Galilee, or Paul's journeys involving the Mediterranean Sea.

Do plants and flowers amaze you? Consider the garden of Eden, the burning bush in the story of Moses, the vine that provided shade for Jonah, the parable of the sower that Jesus told, or the illustration of the vine and the branches that Jesus used in expressing what it looks like to abide in a relationship with Him.

Mountains are my thing, and the Bible is full of them. Much can be learned about God when you read about Mount Sinai (Ex. 19:1-25, 24:12-18; 32:7-16), Mount Zion (Psalm 48, 125, 133), or the sermons Jesus delivered on mountainsides (i.e. Matt. chapters 4-7). Much can be learned about Jesus and people on the mount of transfiguration (Matt. 17:1-9). Much can be revealed about you, other people, and God on Mount Carmel (1 Kings 18:16-46) or the Mount of Olives (Matt. 24-26; Luke 19). You might like the challenge of giving some of these mountains a new name that is personal to your mountain experiences, or come up with names for the mountains spoken of in Psalm 46, 121, or 125.

What about wildlife? The Bible is full of animal stories, starting in the book of Genesis. There is the story of Noah's passengers (Gen. 6-9), Balaam's donkey (Num. 22), the ravens that fed Elijah (1 Kings 17), the sheep under David's care (1 Sam. 16), the lions that were prevented from harming Daniel (Dan. 6), the worm that ate the shade tree in Jonah's story (Jonah 4), and even the colt that Jesus rode into Jerusalem (Mark 11). Consider the examples of wisdom demonstrated in the animal kingdom in the Bible, like the ant in Proverbs 6:6 or the bear in Proverbs 17:12.

Whatever aspect of creation strikes a note with your heart, listen for the voices that declare the glory of God as you read the stories of the Bible. Voices of creation are there for a listening ear, and they have the potential to transform and carry the heart to greener pastures. The voices may not be obvious like a parrot or a crow which can learn to repeat words and mimic language, but a listening heart can see evidence everywhere of God as a supernatural Creator.

Consider the woodchuck. It has an amazing muscular structure in it's ear that prevents even the smallest particle of dust from entering. The woodchuck can dig furiously, moving upwards of 700 pounds of earth in a single season, yet keep clean ears. That kind of design is a voice of creation proclaiming divine construction.

Did you know that the feathery tufts on the head of a great horned owl have nothing to do with hearing?[17] The actual ears are in different locations on each side of the owl's head. Because this offset feature is in place, sounds reach each ear at a different moment. This gives owls the ability to pinpoint, with incredible accuracy, the source of a sound. The ears of a woodcock, on the other hand, are between the eyes and the bill, enabling it to search for worms. These are certainly declarations of intelligent design.

What about hummingbirds? They are so fragile, tiny, and yet beautiful. The tiniest is known as the bee-hummingbird. Just over two inches long, most of it is tail feathers and beak. It weighs about the same as several aspirins, and yet it can hover, moving up and down, sideways, or in and out with amazing flexibility. Somehow the bird, like many of its relatives, knows when to head south and migrate all the way to places like the Panama Canal. In addition, it knows just when to head back and what route to take to arrive at the same destination. Is that by accident? Could it be that these are voices declaring the wonder of Creator design? I hope the question is rhetorical for you.

The black-headed gull can drink either fresh or salt water because of special glands which extract and get rid of salt from the blood. Similar glands above the eyes get rid of excess salt through openings in the bill. That kind of design speaks of more than mere adaptability.

The yellow-shafted flicker is a bird equipped with a long, sticky tongue enabling it to consume thousands of ants.   As a woodpecker, it is also equipped with a sponge-like, rubbery tissue between the beak and cranium. This gives it an amazing capacity to absorb shock as it slams its head against trees hundreds of times a day in search of bugs. None of us would want that calling, but then we are not designed for it. Remind yourself of that the next time you feel like beating your head against the wall. Instead, walk by faith in your Creator according to the unique design He put in you.

Consider the front legs of a honeybee, complete with special hairs serving as a tool to clean the eyes and a joint brush that the bee can pull its antenna through to clean it. What about a beaver's tail that enables it to slap the water as a warning of danger, or to support its body when felling trees, or as a rudder for water travel?

Some of creation's voices declare a fun side that brings a smile to the heart. Have you ever watched otters swimming playfully, doing belly flops, rolls, or sliding down a snow covered slope at high speed for hours? Otters eat fish, but they can also be observed simply playing with fish for the fun of it, releasing them after getting tired of the game.

Have you seen a close-up picture of a shrew? I mean, why does it always have its nose up in the air? Or, have you ever really studied the look of a moose, a camel, or observed two chipmunks in a nose-touching kiss before bouncing on their way? Have you watched a chipmunk fill up its cheeks with food? According to *Character Sketches*, the individual all-time record for a chipmunk's food-carrying ability includes:[18]

- 13 prune stones
- 16 chinquapin nuts
- 31 corn kernels
- 32 beechnuts
- 65 sunflower seeds
- 145 grains of wheat

Picture a chipmunk with a dozen prune stones in its puffed out mouth. What caption might you put on a picture like that? Have fun with it. Be a green voice that declares the wonder of God with a joyful heart.

Creation Groans

With all of the good lessons available through nature's voices, there is also a deep groaning. Creation's cry should be part of our concern. The environment around us is getting more and more dirty and ugly. Every flight I've experienced into Los Angeles was marked by a descent into smog. There are too many rivers where the fish are not safe to eat. Toxic chemicals in the soil. Trash along all of our roadways. I heard once that over seven million cars are junked every year in America. Some states have to pay big money for trash removal and disposal. American families throw away billions of metal cans and glass bottles. Oil spills leave dark images.

The Bible writer captured a reality in the words of Romans 8:

> The creation waits in eager expectation for the sons of God to be revealed. For the creation was subjected to frustration, not by its own choice, but by the will of the one who subjected it, in hope that the creation itself will be liberated from its bondage to decay and brought into the glorious freedom of the children of God. We know that the whole creation has been groaning as in the pains of childbirth right up to the present time (Rom. 8:19-23).

Frustration, freedom, and groaning are human things attributed to a created order that is under a curse. Perhaps *anger* is another word that could be used to further describe the groaning. I was driving by the Susquehanna River after severe floodwaters, and it still looked angry. It seemed to have a distasteful appearance like it had enjoyed the destructive path of days before. Maybe that was reading too much into it, but I know we live in a fallen world with forces that would like to discourage us and even conquer us. It is an angry climate, groaning in expectation for redemption.

I noticed a great deal of cleanup happening after the devastation of flash floods. Many people were reaching out with helping hands to neighbors and friends, building bridges of restoration and hope. That is encouraging, especially when it communicates the message that God is the real source of help and hope. He alone is our refuge and strength, our ever-present help in trouble (Psalm 32:7, 37:39, 46:1, 59:16, 138:7).

I am among those who believe that when we pray "Thy kingdom

come, Thy will be done" (Matt. 6:10), we are asking God to use us as agents of kingdom building reconciliation and restoration. That includes doing our part in stewardship and restoration of the created order in light of the original design. We need to remember that after creating the world, God looked at all He had created and called it "good" (Gen. 1:31). Helping people after destructive floods is good. Helping people restore a devastated environment is redemptive.

Complete restoration will not happen before Jesus Christ returns, but there is a sense in which His kingdom is "already but not yet." Followers of King Jesus are called to be agents of the kingdom of light, walking in the light and bringing light into the world. This will not be fully manifested until Jesus comes as the Light of lights, but Jesus also said "The kingdom is near, at hand (Matt. 4:17; Luke 10:9-11). It is a salvation plan we are invited to be a part of. We are also to pray for it, inviting His kingdom to come.

Part of the groaning and perhaps even the sense of *anger* in creation is because of the presence of evil in our world. There is also a kingdom of darkness.

Looking down into the crater of a huge volcano was a memorable moment when visiting our son at the YWAM (Youth With A Mission) base in Hawaii. The steam vents all around us were reminders of potentially violent activity deep under the earth. A comparison to the work of the Devil is not a stretch. The kingdom of darkness is still vigorously involved in the world, contributing to the groaning of creation. Our hearts were saddened in seeing numerous altars of worship that had been set up at the crater's edge, not to the living God but to some "under the earth god of the volcano."

Rooted in a fear-based desire to appease the spirits deep in the volcano, people had deposited around the edges everything from flowers to fruits and various other gifts. There was even a half empty bottle of Cold Turkey Whiskey. That image is still funny, yet very sad. I wasn't sure whether to laugh or cry. There is an irony in giving to a false god, out of fear, a substance that many ingest as a means to bury fears in a temporary stupor. I remembered the truth that God does not give us a spirit of fear, "But of power, and of love, and of a sound mind" (2 Tim. 1:7).

The immensity of the crater and the expanse of the lava beds pointed to a power beyond imagination. It was a moment of worship for us, that Jesus is Lord of things "above the earth, on and in the earth, and under the earth" (Phil. 2:10-11). Yes, even under the earth. I hope that you are thankful to be a child of the living God, the God of all power, greater than the largest volcano. He is beyond the supernovas of the universe, bigger than any mountain of the earth, yet a God who loved us enough to give His best, His Son, Himself. To participate in creation care and restoration is to declare His sovereignty over all we see, piercing the darkness with His glory.

The Groans of Human Impact

Everything that God created was spoken into existence primarily to glorify Him. Everything that is, both in heaven and on earth, was brought into being mainly to magnify Him and bring honor to His name. It would be wise to give thought to the proposition that we may be selfishly appropriating for our own use what God ordained for His own worship.[19]

When we selfishly use what God ordained for His honor, we fail to glorify Him. When we carelessly use resources He provided rather than honoring Him with our lifestyle, we fail to worship and declare His worth-ship. If our lifestyle leads to destroying the environment, we are interfering and hindering what God created to worship Him. We have the ability to cause groaning in creation.

We do have the capacity and ability to, in the words of Revelation 11:18, "destroy the earth." Throughout history people have made choices that contributed to the scene pictured by the prophet Isaiah, "The waters of Nimrim are dried up, and the grass is withered; the vegetation is gone and nothing green is left" (Isaiah 15:6). Sure, some modern day conclusions and reports are dramatized and overstated, but degradation of the environment is real and visible to any observant eye. The issue of garbage disposal itself is a significant contemporary issue. Visit a third world country and walk the urban beaches. Consider these facts as presented by Calvin B. DeWitt:[20]

> ➤ Since 1850, people have converted over 2.2 billion acres of natural lands to human use. This means deforestation, drainage of wetlands, and destruction of grasslands and prairies.
> ➤ More than three species of plants and animals are extinguished daily.

> ➤ Some 70,000 chemicals have been created by human ingenuity that cannot be absorbed back into the environment, including biocides, pesticides, herbicides, and fungicides.
> ➤ Increased burning exposing carbon-containing materials to oxygen brings rising concentrations of atmospheric carbon dioxide, potentially enhancing the greenhouse effect that has led to the concern of global warming. The melting snow caps, receding glaciers and slowly rising sea level may not be completely blamed on these things; there are certainly cycles in weather and climate. However, it cannot be denied that changes are happening.

It is not clear how much of current environmental issues can be blamed on the activity of man, but it is clear that people can be a part of the solution. In fact, the groaning of creation and the command of the Creator to take care of the garden invite active engagement in a movement that honors God. As Tony Campolo said in his book, *How to Rescue the Earth Without Worshiping Nature*:

> The doctrines of evolution that extolled the power to dominate and to control the resources of nature are doctrines that have contributed greatly to the demise of the earth's well-being. A theologically and biblically based alternative that is harmonious with science could alter the modern consciousness. It could provide an important contribution to a new mind-set that makes living in harmonious cooperation with the rest of nature a dominant virtue. It could help turn things around and reverse the trend toward an ecological apocalypse.[21]

Diversity of Voices

It is actually quite amazing what man can build. The genius of modern architecture is demonstrated in bridges, structures like the Empire State Building, and vessels designed to put men on the moon. There are also many examples before modernity. We can dip way back. What about the tower of Babel written about in Genesis chapter eleven? With one voice they were declaring man's glory, and so their languages were confused because they had lost the most important voice, that of the one and only Creator God.

It is dangerous ground to listen to the voices of modern thinkers who promote humanism and the lie that man can be his own god, a deception described in Genesis 3:1-7. It is also a perilous pursuit to build human towers of thought rooted in worship of *mother earth*. Some of these friends speak of a special communion with nature that promotes them to environmental activism. To build on such teachings is to build on shaky foundations. Wisdom and discernment reveal the distractions and distortions of truth.

The true voices of green in God's creation have outlasted man's attempts to create and build. While serving in the Philippines, we took our boy scout troop to the Island of Corregidor, which sits in the middle of Manila Bay. It has been a strategic place for military purposes throughout the years. The Philippines and U.S. troops lost control of Corregidor to the Japanese in 1941 and captured it back in 1944. It is full of ruins, old blown apart artillery batteries, bombed out barracks, buildings full of war scars, and a massive tunnel system where historical treasures can be found.

Incredible contrast can be observed on the Island. Beautiful plants and jungle rain forest vegetation, flowers, and even orchids thrive in the midst of the rubble and destruction from previous wars. New life is growing in amongst man's ruins. As wonderful and marvelous as the original buildings were, man also has the ability for painful devastation. In the midst of that, God's creation prevails.

This serves as an illustration of how man's best (the island was a first class military base) will fade away in destruction, but the sparrow and lily (representatives of creation) are beautifully relying on God (Matt. 6:25-30). It also illustrates the reality of war, on the surface and beyond what we can see.

There are only two kingdoms in the universe, the kingdom of light (under God's reign) and the kingdom of darkness. The groaning of creation is due in large part to the darkness of sin and evil that are under the dominion of Satan and his demonic realm. We can do much damage on our own, even without the influence of evil, but the truth is that sin and wickedness have perverted nature and darkened God's creation. The Devil does everything he can to lure nature away from the high calling of worship unto the Creator.

So, people who pollute the earth and exercise selfish damage and careless waste should be warned about becoming partners with Satan in destroying the purpose of creation to worship God. Let's be honest.   Greed, littering, waste, careless use of resources, and disregard for nature are one thing---sin. To forsake our responsibility for creation care and to damage the beauty around us is to hinder and limit the worshipful character of the created order. It is unwise to efface or erase the marks of the great Designer, our Creative God. But, there is a hopeful alternative.

One of the scouts on Corregidor Island approached me with an ugly looking seed pod and invited me to open it up. What was an ugly shell revealed the most amazing little black seeds on the inside, with perfectly shaped white hearts on them. It was like someone had painted white hearts on the black seeds, but they were created that way. I still don't know what kind of trees they came from, but it was intriguing. It was a *wow moment*, a *God wink*, a *divine appointment*. Creation is full of those kind of moments for those who take the time to look and listen. The next time your environment seems like a black seed, be a white heart with a green voice of the earth.

Restoration Fruit

The world needs to see the healing of creation that only comes from being in fellowship with God in Christ Jesus. Loving God means loving all that He created. Creation declares the story of God's glory. Creation gives clear evidence of God's eternal power and His love and care for the earth. Many students of the Bible would agree that John 3:16, "For God so loved the world..." could arguably apply to all the world He created. That means people, but also the created world where He places us.

Please note my conviction, as taught in the Bible, that the curse on the earth came as a result of the fall of mankind and with each passing generation this effect upon the creation is magnified.   We need to have a concern about restoration, but kept in the context of a more critical truth. As a wise friend, Dr. Jim Lindsey, wrote in an email to me, "We should have a greater, growing overall sensitivity to our environment, but if we neglect the greater message that is connected to the fall of man and to his continued idolatrous, sinful behavior we will miss the mark in any environmental message we may bring to the forum."[22]

Jim also pointed out Luke 19:10, which highlights the reality of Jesus coming to seek and to save what was lost, or "that" which was lost. It could be argued that lost souls are clearly a part of the issue, but the words indicate "that" which was lost and not just "those who" were lost. When sin came into the world, everything was broken, including creation, and all is in need of restoration and renewal.

God's creation plan focuses on humans created in His image. At the same time, that truth should not be severed from the world in which He breathed life into humankind. Part of His plan, after all, involves the promise of land, a promised land. Consider the Abrahamic covenant. In Genesis chapter twelve, God spoke to Abraham the promise of a land where the seed of a blessed offspring would be fruitful and multiply. That is a perspective from heaven.

Believers in a Creator are to be instruments of restoration. Consider the words of Robert E. Webber:

> The place to begin a study of God's vision for the world is in the Genesis account of creation. In the story of God's activity on each day of creation, we find a vision of how the world once was and what the world will once again become. Between the account of creation and re-creation lie the fall and, of course, God's work in Jesus Christ to rescue and restore the world, fulfilling God's original vision for creation and creatures.[23]

So many things in creation contain imbedded illustrations of the salvation restoration plan. Conflict resolution in literature reveals our common desire to get back to good news. We crave resolution in music. Ending a song on an unfinished note stirs an uneasy tension. We are unsettled deep within when things are left unresolved and peace is not experienced. Jesus spoke to the wind and the sea one day and brought a sense of peace and calm for His disciples. Even the wind and the sea, elements of the created order, obey Him (Matt. 8:23-27). "All things were made through Him, and without Him nothing was made that was made. In Him was life, and the life was the light of men" (John 1:3-4).

The creation account makes it clear that God created a world of order out of chaos. He created order from disorder, and it was of good order. The writer of the Genesis account noted numerous times that God "saw that it was good." (Gen. 1:9, 12, 18, 21, 25).   In fact, "And God saw all that he had made, and it was very good" (Gen. 1:31a). Sin, however, stained, marred and killed. Participating in creation care is joining God in restoring order.   Reminders of the need for restoration surround us.

We can see evidence of God's restoration work every day. He enables things to thrive in the most dire circumstances. Have you ever explored a desert? If you ever drive through such a dry wilderness, you can't help but notice the striking contrast between the very hot and dusty soil (or sand) with some of the unique blossoming desert plant life that does more than survive there.

On a recent trip through Nevada, I reflected on the contrast between being a citizen of heaven and living in this often dry and dusty world. There is an apparent contradiction, perhaps a paradox involved in blooming with life in Christ even in the wilderness. The contrast of fruitful life in Christ against the backdrop of death is most obvious when the circumstances are dusty and resources of the world are dried up. Consider the words of Jesus:

> I am the vine; you are the branches. If a man remains in me and I in him, he will bear much fruit; apart from me you can do nothing. If anyone does not remain in me, he is like a branch that is thrown away and withers; such branches are picked up, thrown into the fire and burned. If you remain in me and my words remain in you, ask whatever you wish, and it will be given you. This is to my Father's glory, that you bear much fruit, showing yourselves to be my disciples (John 15:5-8).

You can abide in Him and gain your strength in Him as you sink your roots deeply into His sustaining life. He delights in producing fruit as a demonstration of the contrast of His indwelling life in a world so overheated by pain and evil. That kind of blooming fruitfulness is all to His glory.

Eating some fruit one recent morning, I was considering the amazing qualities of a banana. It is a remarkable fruit, isn't it? The color reveals its readiness to eat, the unique shape fits well in your hand, and the quick pull tab lends easy access to a delicious treat. Pealing back the layers is like uncovering a tasty mystery.

There is also delicious mystery in how God sometimes reveals fruit through us during tough times in the deserts of life, like desserts in the desert. As the layers of our lives are pealed back, what is deep within gets revealed. It is when Jesus followers are exposed and vulnerable that the fruit of His Spirit can be on display. When the coverings people trust in and the masks they wear are stripped away; when the inner self is uncovered by trying circumstances; when who you really are deep inside is laid out for all to see; there is opportunity for others to witness love, joy, peace, patience, kindness, goodness, faithfulness, gentleness and self control (Gal. 5:22-24). There is no legalistic rule behind that, just the real Jesus.

In the moments when you are most vulnerable and weak, may your heart be one of authenticity and worship. As the songwriter put it so well:

> When the music fades, and all is stripped away
> > And I simply come.
> Longing just to bring, something that's of worth
> > That will bless your heart
> I bring you more than a song.......[24]

Parrot Mountain

On a family vacation, one of the special spots I visited was a place called Parrot Mountain. The owner shared with me the origins of the mountainside parrot paradise. He had experienced a dream, with vivid images, about a marvelous place he later built. He shared his passion for Genesis chapter two, the creation story. He told me his vision, to glorify God by creation displays of birds, plants, and trees, including the providing of a sanctuary for exotic birds.

Many of the birds were in the open on a perch with nothing holding them there. I asked how it was that they didn't fly away. He responded that the key was found in taking care of them, feeding and providing for them. When the birds are cared for, they have no reason to go elsewhere. Training was also a feature, and some birds needed to have their wings slightly clipped, but proper care was the essential ingredient.

The first plaque I came to when walking the path of Parrot

Mountain said this:

> And the Lord God planted a Garden eastward in Eden; and there He put the man who he had formed. And out of the ground made the Lord God to grow every tree that is pleasant to the sight, and good for food; the tree of life also in the midst of the garden, and the tree of knowledge of good and evil. And the Lord God took the man, and put him into the garden of Eden to dress it and to keep it.[25]

I also enjoyed time in a lush prayer garden with a waterfall marked by a powerful Bible reference, "The Lord will guide you always; he will satisfy your needs in a sun-scorched land and will strengthen your frame. You will be like a well-watered garden, like a spring whose waters never fail" (Isaiah 58:11).

It was a wonderful, peaceful spot. There is an even greater well-watered garden, sustained in never ending supply, a place more than green. It is described with a powerful voice in the last book of the Bible:

> Then the angel showed me the river of the water of life, as clear as crystal, flowing from the throne of God and of the Lamb down the middle of the great street of the city. On each side of the river stood the tree of life, bearing twelve crops of fruit, yielding its fruit every month. And the leaves of the tree are for the healing of the nations. No longer will there be any curse. The throne of God and of the Lamb will be in the city, and his servants will serve him. They will see his face, and his name will be on their foreheads. There will be no more night. They will not need the light of a lamp or the light of the sun, for the Lord God will give them light. And they will reign for ever and ever. (Rev. 22:1-5)

The grace of God is equal to the most uncongenial
temperaments and to the most unfavorable circumstances.
~A.B. Simpson~

For Reflection/Discussion:

1. Read Revelation 21-22. What appeals to you about the description of a new heaven, a new earth, and a restored heavenly garden?
2. Read Isaiah 35:1-2 and reflect on a time when you have had to bloom where you were planted, when the circumstances tempted you to do otherwise.
3. What are the obstacles to joy in this season of your life?
4. Share an experience in your journey that was like an oasis in the desert.
5. What evidence do you see around you that indicates the planet is broken? Where have you observed "groaning" in nature around you?
6. What have you observed in creation that shows evidence of evil?
7. What plant or animal has been a "green voice" that aroused your curiosity? What might you learn about God?

Chapter 6

Stewarding

The Lord God took the man and put him in the Garden of Eden
to work it and take care of it.
~Genesis 2:15~

You were created for worship and fellowship with God, a working relationship like the first humans had in the Garden of Eden. God loves people, and He provides a way for us to join in His creative and re-creative work through this thing we call stewardship.

This is a key word for a true green mentality. I recently passed a billboard on the road that declared, "Even mother nature has an agent, STEWARDSHIP. Pass it on." Those who embrace the truth of God as the Creator (not *mother nature*) have the highest motive to participate in stewardship that demonstrates creation care.

Consider the words of Psalm 8:

> When I consider your heavens, the work of your fingers,
>> the moon and the stars, which you have set in place,
>> what is man that you are mindful of him,
>> the son of man that you care for him?
> You made him a little lower than the heavenly beings
>> and crowned him with glory and honor.
> You made him ruler over the works of your hands;
>> you put everything under his feet:
>>> all flocks and herds,
>>> and the beasts of the field,
>>> the birds of the air,
>>> and the fish of the sea,
>>> all that swim the paths of the seas.
> O Lord, our Lord, how majestic is your name in all the earth!
>> (Psalm 8:3-9)

This is a wonderful passage providing solid foundations for biblical stewardship. If we truly consider God's handiwork, everything that He has set in place, we feel smaller in light of His majesty. Yet, mankind is the apex and focal point of God's creation.[26] He made us ruler over creation, rule being properly understood, to take care of His creatures. When we realize this as the contribution we are invited to participate in, we proclaim with more than our lips that He is majestic in all the earth.

To neglect God's creation is to abandon the charge He has given us. Because He reveals Himself through the work of His hands (Rom. 1:20), to abuse and harm creation hinders components of His revelation to us. Acts of worship through creation care, on the other hand, are powerful. It means embracing, in humility, the truth of who we are and whose we are as people created in His image. That bleeds into sacrificial living in order to rule in creation with proper honor and respect.

Stewardship Trails

If you are a follower of Jesus, the journey you are on is marked by wonderful mysteries of truth that God has entrusted to you. That includes creation lessons all around you. You are a steward of the mysteries of God, and it is required of stewards that they be found trustworthy (1 Cor. 4:1-2).

Hiking out of the wilderness, my son and I were working our way down a ravine toward the main trail. We were using a map and compass to get out of the high country toward home. There were no obvious well-traveled trails to follow, but there were some narrow game trails where others had gone before. Although tough to track, these remnants of previous travel provided a safe passage.

As long as we focused on the trail, the walking was relatively easy.   However, we were often distracted by the scenery or the terrain and too easily lost sight of the path.   That made the going tougher. Sometimes we ended up in thorny thickets. Once, Colter stepped onto a moss bed that ended up being a bog, sucking him knee-deep into the slime. Losing sight of the path created difficult consequences, but rediscovering the trail was a source of renewed energy for the journey.

Proverbs chapter fifteen has something interesting to say here, "The way of the sluggard is blocked with thorns, but the path of the upright is a highway." And in verse twenty one, "Folly delights a man who lacks judgment, but a man of understanding keeps a straight course."

It would be good for God to block those sluggard times with thorns, keeping us on His highway, the course less traveled but right. We need the eyes of understanding to stay on the Creator's trails, where He has taken others before. Each of us leaves footprints as we journey, and it would be wonderful if all who come behind find us faithful stewards.

Rejoice in God's provisions of and for the earth. Singing on the trail of stewardship is encouraged.

> You will go out in joy and be led forth in peace; the mountains and hills will burst into song before you, and all the trees of the field will clap their hands. Instead of the thornbush will grow the pine tree, and instead of briers the myrtle will grow. This will be for the Lord's renown, for an everlasting sign, which will not be destroyed" (Isaiah 55:12-13).

Needs or Wants?

Stewardship of resources includes coming to recognize the distinction between wants and needs. If we service every want and use every resource with unsustainable cravings, we cannot be effective in stewardship. Not only that, but lack of concern makes us part of the problem and not part of the solution. A materialistic mindset that satisfies every craving is not healthy for us, for others, or for the world in which we live. Materialistic spirituality cannot and will not ever satisfy. Stewardship is an act of worship to the Creator, and that includes sacrifice that avoids scratching every itch.

I picked up poison oak somewhere. I wanted to dig my fingernails in and scratch to my heart's delight. Unrestrained scratching of the itches would have caused more damage. I discovered during an early morning walk that physical exercise really helped. The activity served to both increase my will power and offer a better focus. The inspiration of God's creation, talking with my wife, and prayer patterned with forward progress brought great relief and significantly readjusted my itchy desires. The effects didn't bother me when I was busy with productive activity.

There are other ailments where scratching the itch is the worst thing you could do. Cuts, sunburn, dengue fever, and the itches of various sinful temptations cause further damage if you give in to the urges. It takes self discipline to ignore what you'd love to do for relief. It is in that battleground of the mind where God's power is manifested and character is built. As Paul wrote in his letter, "For physical training is of some value, but godliness has value for all things, holding promise for both the present life and the life to come" (1 Tim. 4:8). That includes embracing the godliness of sustainable living and sacrificial stewardship.

There are so many ways that we as humans waste resources because of the drive of wants over needs. If we were decisive about using what we need rather than what we want, would it make a difference?

Atmospheric Stewardship

You probably know that Isaac Newton (1642 – 1727) is famous for his discovery of the law of universal gravitation and the formulation of the three laws of motion. Newton also wrote some inspiring truth when he declared, "We account the Scriptures of God to be the most sublime philosophy. I find more sure marks of authenticity in the Bible than in any profane history whatsoever."[27]

That is the kind of truth that kept Newton moving with purpose for a significant impact. He believed, like millions of others, that the Bible is fact and what is said about the Creator is true. The greatest rule of motion is found in the book of Acts, "For in him we live and move and have our being" (Acts 17:28). That is authentic and life giving truth. That is gravitational stability that keeps us moving.

Our atmosphere, because of the physics of gravity, is an amazing source of protection and a resource for life. This includes the wonders of global circulations of water and air essential to existence. Without the atmosphere, the sun would eventually destroy us. The sun pours out immense energy in all directions and energizes everything on the earth. All life, ocean currents, winds, storms, and animals get energy provided by the sun. It is the atmosphere around the earth that filters out the dangerous rays so that we are protected and so that the right light is delivered to the surface of our planet.

Ozone, a component of our atmosphere, has a particular value for us. Without the protection of our atmospheric ozone, ultraviolet radiation would be lethal. That radiation from the sun can destroy chemical bonds that hold molecules together and break up that DNA that is vital for life. It is the filtered light of the sun which makes life possible, bringing forth crops and resources to be harvested and stewarded.

Water vapor, carbon dioxide, and other greenhouse gases trap energy and delay some of its return to space as reflected light. The earth therefore becomes energized and warm, but not explosive or too warm. That is another proclamation of grand design, and bids us to engage in proper stewardship practices that will sustain these components of the air.

All of this declares the incredible creative power of the God of creation. As the psalmist wrote it, "He wraps himself in light as with a garment; he stretches out the heavens like a tent" (Psalm 104:2). Part of that tent is kept by the provision of gravity in the earth's incredible plan inviting us to care.

It is often the simple things that help us to cultivate grateful hearts that have moved beyond mere environmentalism. Whenever I take a detour to pick up trash in my path because I care about creation, it is an act of worship. Taking pleasure in watering a plant is appreciation for God's green earth. A trip to the recycling center is a way to be a good steward as an act of gratitude. Being sensitive of what I put into the air is honorable. Walking in an attitude of creation care and meaningful stewardship is a walk of worship.

Oceans Green

Somewhere around seventy percent of the earth is covered by ocean. Although there is plenty of evidence of a worldwide flood that covered the earth at one time, receding waters at the hand of God brought forth life on land and in the sea. The ocean can easily be a forgotten place in need of stewarding, but the ocean was God's idea. Consider the continued words of Psalm 104:

He set the earth on its foundations;
    it can never be moved.
You covered it with the deep as with a garment;
    the waters stood above the mountains.
But at your rebuke the waters fled,
    at the sound of your thunder they took to flight;
        they flowed over the mountains,
        they went down into the valleys,
    to the place you assigned for them.
You set a boundary they cannot cross;
    never again will they cover the earth (Psalm 104:5-9).

It is noteworthy to mention that God set a boundary between land and sea. Part of our stewardship, therefore, is the care for that boundary. Beaches, beachfronts, and shorelines are important places. Although bad storms can breach those borders, we are responsible to do what we can to maintain these transitional ecosystems.

Beaches and shorelines are wonderful places that give us hints about the vastness of the ocean, and sometimes creatures end up there that need our stewardship. I watched a video once which celebrated a group of people who helped redirect a pod of dolphins who had beached themselves, getting them back out to sea. I've been to beaches where sections were roped off to protect the eggs deposited by sea turtles. These are good practices.

I heard the story of a boy who was picking up starfish from a massive group of the amazing creatures who had been washed up on the beach. A man commented to him that he could not possibly make a difference and help all those starfish, there were too many. As the boy threw another one back out into the ocean, he made the comment, "I made a difference for this one." That is good creation care, making a difference one step at a time.

There are resources in the oceans yet to be discovered. As the psalmist wrote, "There is the sea, vast and spacious, teeming with creatures beyond number — living things both large and small. There the ships go to and fro, and the leviathan, which you formed to frolic there" (Psalm 104:25-26). Don't you love the image of a leviathan moving with a frolic? Resources in the ocean for our enjoyment abound like gifts waiting to be opened, but good stewardship opens them with care.

I worked for a season for Land Lindbergh, son of Charles Lindbergh, the famous historical pilot. Land owned and operated a cattle ranch in Greenough, Montana. He gave me a book written by his mother, Anne Morrow Lindbergh, in which she wrote:

> One never knows what chance treasures these easy unconscious rollers may toss up, on the smooth white sand of the conscious mind; what perfectly rounded stone, what rare shell from the ocean floor. Perhaps a channeled whelk, a moon shell, or even an Argonaut. But it must not be sought for---heaven forbid—dug for. No, no dredging of the sea-bottom here. That would defeat one's purpose. The sea does not reward those who are too anxious, too greedy, or too impatient. To dig for treasures shows not only impatience and greed, but lack of faith. Patience, patience, patience, is what the sea teaches. Patience and faith. One should lie empty, open, choiceless as a beach---waiting for a gift from the sea.[28]

Gifts from the sea might show up in unexpected ways for the waiting heart. The gift might be a manifestation of God's power. When God wanted to prove His sovereign caring supremacy, He took Job on a walk through the majesty of His creation. He basically asked him, " could you or anyone else have done all this?"

> Who shut up the sea behind doors
>> when it burst forth from the womb,
> when I made the clouds its garment
>> and wrapped it in thick darkness,
> when I fixed limits for it
>> and set its doors and bars in place,
> when I said, 'This far you may come and no farther;
>> here is where your proud waves halt'? (Job 38:8-11).

I mean, have you ever watched the ocean waves when they were so large that you could feel the power behind them? The shores are a true blessing even in terms of stopping the waves from damage on the coastlands of where life meets the sea in a band of rocks or sand. Be patient. Perhaps a gift from the sea will present you with a stewarding opportunity.

Fresh Water Cycles

A foundational aspect of good creation stewardship is a growing appreciation for the environment and all that it has to offer along with all that it can teach us about God and ourselves. If there are lessons to be learned in the created order, those lessons are assets to be stewarded.

Take water, for example. Water is an amazing substance. Consider what the psalm writer had to say about it:

> He makes springs pour water into the ravines;
>> it flows between the mountains.
> They give water to all the beasts of the field;
>> the wild donkeys quench their thirst.
> The birds of the air nest by the waters;
>> they sing among the branches.
> He waters the mountains from his upper chambers;
>> the earth is satisfied by the fruit of his work.
> (Psalm 104:10-13)

When water percolates into the ground, it is filtered through soil and rock and enters the water table, resulting in accessible drinkable water for our homes. We can learn from that. Many water purification plants use the same system, letting it percolate through beds of sand. This is a marvelous design, especially considering the fact that water is known to be nearly a universal solvent, able to dissolve practically anything. Yet, rather than picking up impurities from sand and rock in the earth it somehow is filtered to become clean water for us to use. Creation's natural distillers, filters, and extractors are perfectly designed as a powerful provision of pure water for life.

Water demonstrates a profound example of recycling. Animals drink it, and water is released into the atmosphere through breathing, sweating, and waste. H_2O then finds its way into the atmosphere or through sewage treatment back into rivers and streams. Plants then take it up through their roots and pump it into stems and leaves which give it back to the atmosphere through transpiration and evaporation. That moisture joins water evaporated from various bodies of water to form rain and snow, re-watering the face of the earth. What a marvelous cycle which includes transformation of water into various forms. Understanding this kind of cycle helps us to become better equipped as instruments of conservation and protection of this valuable resource.

The number of cycles in creation is amazing. Consider the carbon cycle. Carbon dioxide is breathed out by us (along with raccoons, bears, lizards, and other critters) and enters the atmosphere to become the carbon-based stuff of life. This includes the transfer to even microscopic life that depends on it for food. These creatures later return the carbon back to the atmosphere both through their breathing and their own death and decomposition. Water cycles are intimately involved in all of this.

So, even the idea of recycling is not man's invention, nature started it. Recycling began with the very systems God deposited in the created order. Good stewardship invites us to exercise positive influence in these cycles.

Water is a resource that we so easily take for granted. I have heard reports that water is one of those valuable resources that could cause conflicts between countries, even fights and wars. Water rights, water availability, and water consumption are areas of potential quarrels as populations increase and as droughts occur with various weather and climate changes. Learning how to conserve, recycle, and maintain water is a significant issue that will become even more important in the years ahead.

The Animal Kingdom

We can learn much from the animal kingdom. Stewardship of the animal kingdom can be fueled by an attentive appreciation for the wonder found there. It is in creation that "the birds make their nests; the stork has its home in the pine trees. The high mountains belong to the wild goats; the crags are a refuge for the coneys" (Psalm 104:17-18). Squirrels are also one of the inhabitants I'm thinking of these days.

We had fun trying to keep the squirrels out of our bird feeder. I had the feeder hanging from a rope tied to the branch of a large tree, far enough off the ground to prevent the critters from getting to it. I decided to isolate the feeder from them after watching a squirrel hanging on the feeder, not eating the seeds but scooping them out onto the ground with intense energy for all of his friends and family to enjoy. It only took him a few minutes to empty out the feeder.

So, I was certain that hanging a rope from a branch would do the trick. I watched. The squirrels jumped from the tree onto the feeder like they were enjoying a park swing set. So, I tied the feeder to a higher branch with a longer rope, further from the trunk of the tree. I was sure that would do it.

I watched a squirrel scurry down the rope to the feeder like it had just completed obstacle course training in the critter army. I countered by changing from a rope to a wire. Surely they would not be able to grip and slide down a wire. I was wrong. They learned how to slip and slide. Are you smiling yet?

My next strategy was to form a metal cone over the feeder so that they could slide down all they wanted but they would not be able to get a grip onto the feeder. I was unaware of the incredible acrobatic skills of the bushy tailed creatures.

I decided to have some fun with the battle. I smeared grease on the wire, all the way from the top, an entire tube of it. I couldn't resist waiting around to watch them slide uncontrollably down the wire with a shocked landing on the soft grass below. I watched a squirrel sniff at the wire, touch it, then grab on with all fours and slide down the wire faster than ever before. I imagined a smile on his face as he glanced in my direction, happily sliding down the wire. He reached the bird feeder with incredible athletic ability.

The squirrel war actually changed my heart into an appreciation for the delightful critters. A friend said that the best solution was to take videos of the squirrels, post them for sale on the internet, and use the proceeds to purchase more bird seed. That seemed like a good idea, perhaps a bit squirrelly.

May I cast some seeds your direction? The animal kingdom is an amazing source of inspiration in terms of learning how to use resources creatively. The diversity of life in our world is remarkable. We can learn volumes from the millions of different species of living creatures.

Did you know that the first successful production of paper from wood pulp was the result of studies of how wasps made their nests? Have you ever seen a picture of a snipe eel that can live over a mile below the surface of the ocean? What about the anglerfish that can thrive up to 9,800 feet deep? Talk about adaptation and wise use of resources in difficult environments…we could learn from creation.

Have you ever owned a goose-down pillow? Down feathers have been highly valued over the years as excellent insulators of warmth. They have a remarkable ability to lock in heat, part of the design for female geese to help incubate their eggs. When an egg is laid, the goose plucks out some of the down feathers on her breast and places them around the eggs. This actually leaves a bare spot referred to as the "incubation patch."

There are more than 1.5 million kinds of insects that display the wonderful diversity of life. The honey bee is one of my favorites. They build little cities with thousands of cells for honey and larvae, with a special chamber for the queen. I was fascinated when I learned that when warm temperatures inside the hive threaten the honey, squads of bees position themselves at the entrance with fast-beating wings to provide a cooling system. There must be something we can learn from that.

Creation reveals the work of God. Plants and animals are referred to as God's works in Psalm 104. "How many are your works, O Lord! In wisdom you made them all; the earth is full of your creatures. There is the sea, vast and spacious, teeming with creatures beyond number, living things both large and small" (Psalm 104:24-25). Stewardship includes being God's hands to provide for His creation, including animals.

Growing in appreciation for the creatures of creation begins with an attitude of gratitude, but application is needed. Perhaps you'd like to start initiatives of your own to raise the awareness of issues and engage opportunities to do something practical. Creation care is a gospel concern because people are the focal point of creation, but that does in no way give humans the right to trample the animal kingdom without concern.

Some of the most committed people in this realm are related to the hunting and fishing industry. We will consider this further in a later chapter about hunting. There are many human resources being poured into taking care of the created order by outdoorsmen, and not just to improve the quality of hunting. When game management practices are done with excellence and wisdom, it exemplifies good stewardship and it is to the benefit of entire ecosystems.

The Garden

Green is a warm color, a color of growth and health. I'm told that one of the best colors for a presentation background is green. It communicates peace and life. Some say that the color relaxes the mind and offers a refreshing, soothing sense of harmony. Maybe this is because it is the most pervasive color in the natural world. Maybe because there is a deep connection with the original garden of God's creation.

In that place the Bible calls Eden, God created a fruitful world and put man there to enjoy it, take care of it, and partake of the pleasures of that lush place. The Bible talks about many resources that were put in place that we should both utilize and care for. He has even given us the ability to plant and harvest the fruit of our labors, but the growth is credited to Him alone.

> He makes grass grow for the cattle,
>   and plants for man to cultivate —
> bringing forth food from the earth:
>   wine that gladdens the heart of man,
> Oil to make his face shine,
>   and bread that sustains his heart.
> The trees of the Lord are well watered,
>   the cedars of Lebanon that he planted.
>   (Psalm 104:14-16)

I like the description of King Uzziah in the Bible, "…and he had farmers and vinedressers in the hills and in the fertile lands, for he loved the soil." Although it didn't end well for him because he became proud and angry, he was among the ranks of many in the Bible who maintained a love for the garden. This hints of the original intent. God desired the first humans to enjoy the garden. Gardens of kings and palace gardens are recurring terms in the Bible (Jer. 52:7; Neh. 3:15; Esther 7:7). There is a green line from Adam and Eve to Uzziah and other kings to you.

Even on the earth itself, there is such an immense number of plants and animals that one book cannot contain them all. There are over 250,000 flowering plants alone. As John Ray put it so well, "So the Almighty discovers more of his wisdom in forming such a vast multitude of different sorts of creatures, and all with admirable art, than if he had created but a few; for this declares the greatness and unbounded capacity of his understanding."[29]   As Paul wrote in Romans chapter one, creation manifests the eternal attributes of God, His eternal and infinite power, seen in everything in the created order.

There is something special about watching things grow, but gardening is work. It takes effort to till the soil, fertilize the plot, plant the seeds, water the plants, and pull weeds. Doing things like composting is a great form of recycling that contributes to gardening. Such activity manifests good creation care, but not without labor. Friends who are active gardeners would agree, but they would also express the delightful reward that comes with the harvest.

What if you live in a city? A relative of mine is having a tremendous impact with a business that helps people enter the world of urban gardening. Many metropolitan areas are promoting gardening initiatives.   Cities like Philadelphia with their Tree Tenders and Tree Vitalize programs are restoring areas with depleted tree canopies. Why? For one reason, as captured in the words of David Nowak, in a USDA Forest Service Study, "Each of us inhales 35 pounds of oxygen daily, all from plants. Every day, we need seven trees to convert our carbon dioxide to oxygen." Trees and other plants help remove pollution, help with energy costs by serving as shade and windbreaks, and even add to the aesthetic value of real estate.

Health specialists indicate that there are even benefits to recovery and stress reduction with the presence of plants and trees. As David Nowak wrote, "Hospital patients with views of trees recovered ten percent more quickly from surgery and required fewer painkillers than those without the view."[30]   Roger S. Ulrich also contributes well with his words, "People watching natural scenes recovered from stress faster and more completely than those who saw urban scenes without trees."[31]

Things like gardening and tree restoration require wisdom, commitment, an understanding of the issues, and hard work. Part of creation care includes the support of and involvement in research and studies like botany, agriculture, zoology, etc. I have relatives who have studied in such fields, and contributions are being made that benefit creation.

During our time on the Iowa farm over the Christmas holidays one year, we walked a section of what they call *government acres*. These are plots of land that remain untilled, left in their natural state for both economic and environmental reasons. The government provides subsidy to farmers who set aside such acreage.

The area we plodded our way through was overgrown with weeds and tall grass. We were hoping to scare up some of those amazing multi colored pheasants. We saw none of the birds, probably because the vegetation was really thick with the wrong kinds of grasses. My nephew talked about their plan to burn the field in order to revitalize it. He said that certain seeds from good grasses which produce a quality food source will only germinate and grow after freezing and even after the intense heat provided by a fire.

That sounds like something we could all be encouraged by. The best crop of fruit in our lives might be germinated through trials, fires, even frozen wilderness experiences. If tough times will help germinate good fruit in God's hands, that is a good thing. If taking care of creation is a difficult challenge, that is also a good thing. The hard work of stewardship bears fruit that impacts broadly.

Green Fog

I went on a prayer jog early one morning, out to the end of the ridge we lived on. Looking down off the mountain, I spent some time watching the fog in the valley. It was moving along like it was trying to escape the rising sun.

Some say that life is full of mountains and valleys, ups and downs, good times and bad times. Actually, maybe we always have a little of both realms.

Maybe it's about perspective. There is always some fog, and there is always the elevated view. From the heights you can see the fog, and from the fog you know by faith that there is a higher outlook beyond the immediate struggles. Sometimes the fog overshadows the mountaintop with trials and troubles, but always with the hope of higher places. The elevated attitude determines spiritual altitude.

Those living in the mountains know that foggy valleys are frequent occurrences, but the rising sun usually burns it away. At other times the fog is on the mountains and not in the valleys. Foggy or sunshine valleys, foggy mountains, sunshine mountaintops, some of both all the time, that is the journey. What we need is a higher viewpoint.

Wisdom is latching on to God's point of view.

The problem with fog is that you can't see beyond it. The dreary mist hangs on you like a blanket of depression, yet the sun is up there somewhere. It always is, every day. In the western states, valley fog in the morning often means that it is going to be a clear, sunny day. The fog isn't forever. Eventually the sun breaks through to push away the gloom. It takes deeper faith to press on in the radiant warmth of God's presence and God's perspective when you can't see the shining sun. Here is a bright reminder for you, "For the Lord God is a sun and shield" (Psalm 83:11).

If you're in a fog today, God is the answer. If stewarding of God's creation seems like a foggy issue full of misty uncertainties, God our Creator is the answer. Talking about the needs of the oceans, the plant and animal kingdoms, and water resources can be an overwhelming haze. God loves and cares for us enough to give us work to do in being part of the solution that points to His redemption plan. There is so much need in the world around us that you cannot be the entire solution, but you can be a part of it. And God would never ask us to do anything that He is not also willing to empower us to accomplish it for His glory.

Stewardship is Work

It should be noted that when God instructed the first humans to work the garden and take care of it, work was a blessing. The initial command was extended before disobedience brought sin and the curse into the created order. Working the garden and stewarding the resources was a privilege. It was an honorable, blessed, enjoyable activity that was marked by fellowship with the Creator who had worked to make it all.

I was sitting by the campfire reading a commentary by Michael Card on Luke, what he calls the *Gospel of Amazement*. A little ant, a fascinating creature created by an amazing God, crawled across the page like he wanted to make a comment. It's too bad that the ant would not be aware of the statement made about him in the book of Proverbs. Ants are mentioned as one of the four things that are small but extremely wise. Ponder that...ants used as an example of being wise? "Ants are creatures of little strength, yet they store up their food in the summer" (Prov. 30:25). Or, with similar words, "Go to the ant, you sluggard; consider its ways and be wise! It has no commander, no overseer or ruler, yet it stores its provisions in summer and gathers its food at harvest" (Prov. 6:6-8). When the weather is good and food is available, they work hard to store for seasons ahead.

Ants don't speak, but their activity declares divine fingerprints of wisdom on the pages of life. They may be small creatures, but they reveal God's bigger perspective. That is wisdom. That is insight into God's point of view. Their work illustrates good economic counsel, but also profound spiritual lessons for the heart.

The Creator of the ant is even more the Creator of you, and you are amazing. You are "God's workmanship, created in Christ Jesus to do good works, which God prepared in advance for us to do" (Eph. 2:10). Walking in those works as a servant of Christ is wise. It is storing up for the future. We are invited to serve a working God (Gen. 2:2; John 17:4; Rom. 8:28; Eph. 2:2) who calls us to join Him in work to bring Him glory.

Stewardship is work that benefits us now, but it is also storage strategy, with mysterious and amazing future benefit to come. It is expressed in the Bible, "Do not store up for yourselves treasures on earth, where moth and rust destroy, and where thieves break in and steal. But store up for yourselves treasures in heaven, where moth and rust do not destroy, and where thieves do not break in and steal. For where your treasure is, there your heart will be also" (Matt. 6:19-21).

Taking care of the environment requires effort, but it is wonderful and honorable work. The sixth century monastic leader, Benedict, emphasized stewardship of the created order. He insisted on integrating scholarly work with manual labor as a form of creation care.[32] The Psalmist wrote, "Then man goes out to his work, to his labor until evening" (Psalm 104:23). Those words were written in the context of the glory of God in creation. The time to take up the banner is now. Ante up.

*Sing to God, sing praise to his name, extol him who
rides on the clouds —
his name is the LORD — and rejoice before him."*
~Psalm 68:4~

For Reflection/Discussion:

1. Psalm 90 states, "May the favor of the Lord our God rest upon us; establish the work of our hands for us — yes, establish the work of our hands" (Psalm 90:17). What creation care work might God be wanting to do through you? What are your "next steps" to being a better steward of creation and an agent of restoration?

2. Talk about the ways you have observed resources being wasted without respect or concern for creation.

3. What do you need to leave alone as an act of better stewardship? What are your wants versus your needs?

4. Consider the list of ideas for creation care in the appendix. What might you add? What idea might you suggest to your church or organization?

5. How do you know when concern for creation stewardship has crossed the line and gone too far?

6. If other people were to grade you on a scale of 1-10 regarding your stewardship practices, what number would they pick?

7. How do you see materialism as a problem? What are some solutions?

"He was a bold man who first ate an oyster."
~Jonathan Swift~

Chapter 7

Cross Shadows

*If anyone would come after me, he must deny himself
and take up his cross and follow me.*
~Mark 8:34~

One of my struggles with the historic theory of evolution is that it puts power on the throne and superiority in the position of victory. Conflict that results in domination and survival is seen as a desirable quality adding to the progress of a species. The idea of natural selection celebrates the power to overcome enemies like climate and predators which threaten. Plenty of evidence suggests that natural selection is a reality. However, is it possible that this was not the original design?

The teaching that revolves around "survival of the fittest" has infected many veins of culture and creation, including the behavior of people who want to "climb to the top" of the social chain. Reality TV shows can even be accused of feeding the idea that "survivors" do whatever it takes to come out on top, even if it excludes or hurts other people.

If we believe that the created order is groaning, and getting worse, what if the answer lies in love rather than domination and control? What if the solution for all that ails the environment is found in love for God as expressed in loving His creation? Can that be done through sacrificial living that honors God by loving the people who are the central concern in God's redemptive plan?

One of the questions asked about Christianity is why Jesus had to die on a cross. For sure, it can be said that sin and disobedience are that bad. Taking care of the worst problem imaginable took the worst kind of death penalty imaginable. The fall talked about in Genesis chapter three was such a destructive whirlwind that it took the worst form of punishment to deal with it and provide a way to set things right. To reduce the meaning of the cross in any way is to try to reduce the holiness and glory of God. If we try to make the cross smaller we are trying to make God less than the perfect, holy, hallowed Father He is. God is infinite and perfect. We are finite and fallen. Our only hope is a perfect Savior with no sin of His own to pay for taking upon Himself the debt we owe.

The substitutionary sacrifice of Jesus on the cross is the greatest act of love. He loves you and me enough to take the penalty in our place, expressing an act of amazing, incomprehensible love. It is the reason I became a follower of God. What He did and what He does deserves my life as a "thank you" note unto the God of the universe who creates and redeems. I live in the shadow of the cross.

Images of the cross can be discovered by the inquisitive eye in nature itself. Consider Laminins, a protein that is essential for the health of humans and animals alike. Do a google image search sometime on the word, "Laminin." See the cross.

Skeptics would cry "fowl" to such imagery, and it is certainly not wise to carry anything in creation too far. Everything should be analyzed and considered in light of the truth of the Bible without crossing the line into faulty hermeneutics. That being said, the message of the cross can be discovered all over the created world.

When hiking with a friend, we talked about the shadow of the cross that is a strong part of all Christian thought. On the trail we spoke of the Father's view of us, the shadow cast from His radiance to us through the cross. We reflected on how He sees us through Jesus and HIS cross, if we will believe on Him. I remember the day I received Christ and His forgiveness, and invited His Lordship in my life. I was forgiven and adopted into His upright family. I was given life in the shadow of a redemption secured on a hill of death outside of Jerusalem.

In the shadow of the cross I find the true Christ-life and its every blessing, flowing from His heart, from His outstretched arms in that expression of incredible love. As we consider the cross and gaze in the beautiful, caring face of Jesus, we see not just the shadow---- but the radiance beyond.

The sunrise was beautiful that day of hiking. We were surrounded by God's handiwork. As the afternoon advanced toward evening, the shadows cast by the setting sun grew longer. In similar fashion, the shadow of the cross expands as the sun sets on history. God is advancing His kingdom and many people have entered into His path, taking up the cross to follow Him.

Fall Shadows

I experienced the presence of God with some thankful reflection as I jogged along a trail recently, enjoying the beautiful fall scenery. The autumn leaves provided an amazing vista of colors, and it required very little effort to soak in the beauty. Autumn is a wonderful season. The colorful trees declare God's glory as they display shades of transformation. Soon they will do something definitive and profound; they will finish the process of death and fall to the ground to become mulch that helps resource new life.

Jesus said, "If anyone would come after me, he must deny himself and take up his cross and follow me. For whoever wants to save his life will lose it, but whoever loses his life for me will find it" (Matt. 16:24-26). Paul wrote to the Colossians, "Put to death, therefore, whatever belongs to your earthly nature....." (Col. 3:5). Self denial and self sacrifice, dying to our own selfish desires, is a beautiful thing because it is a source of greater life.

In God's economy, the process of self denial and dying to self is very colorful and attractive. This process can be noted throughout the created order. Seeds of all variety display death in order to facilitate life. The death of organisms provides nutrients for new life. The transformation of green foliage to autumn colors and then to brown death is a remarkable image of God's plan.

When people put others first and deny themselves, that is greater than the colors of autumn. Self sacrifice is a contagious resource for abundant life. Christ followers who live out of this truth appreciate the beauty of transformation, like a snapshot of mixed colors portraying death unto life. The process of self denial brings forth an attractive panorama that beautifies our landscape and facilitates new life for others.

When a mom sacrifices her own schedule to take care of her children, that is a striking color that multiplies life. When a husband gives up something he wants to do in order to get interested in something his wife likes, that is more than a colorful bouquet.

When an elderly woman sings a contemporary song in church that she doesn't necessarily like, but she joins in enthusiastically for the encouragement of community, that is stunning. When a grieving person reaches out to others who are hurting, the colors dazzle the heart. When a teen helps with the ministry of the church rather than expecting to be entertained, that is eye-catching. When someone going through a rough time shows up at church even though they don't feel like being there, others are encouraged by those colors of personal sacrifice. When a busy couple gives a Sunday morning in the nursery or Children's church, the gratitude of parents adds to the array of living art. When people step into the grace of giving, sharing even beyond what they are able, the colors of God's glory sparkle with His radiant presence. When people give of their time and energy to clean up a field in our Father's garden, that is self-sacrificing worship.

Christians often talk about the value of thinking outside of themselves; the act of being selfless in service to other people is often valued as an act of worship. Acting selfless in care of the creation God has entrusted to us can be celebrated in the same way. Composting organic waste and reusing it for gardening is not simply a new-age trend, it is an act of worship that brings us in touch with the brilliance of God's creation. The death and decomposition of one thing brings life to another. Everywhere around us these tiny mysteries of sacrifice can be seen. When we take the time to notice them, the grandeur of our creator becomes more and more apparent. Too often, we busy ourselves and miss the opportunity to appreciate the little things packed with life and death lessons.

Even greater than the colors of trees in the fall are the colors of the selfless life, declaring the glory of God. People who deliberately take an interest in caring for God's creation are colorful people. When people sacrifice by living within their means to preserve God's resources and the environment, wonderful shades of deep green are displayed.

Jesus said it best, "If anyone would come after me, he must deny himself and take up his cross daily and follow me" (Luke 9:23). "I die daily" (1 Cor. 15:31). Worshipful creation stewards walk beyond green revealing the cross and a resurrected, new creation life (Gal. 6:15).

Fertile Fall

The plethora of colors in the fall is wonderful, but after the delightful views start to trail off the dead leaves begin coming down.

Is that why they call it fall, because that is what the leaves do? The death of leaves produces mulch and fertilizer for soil production which will contribute to new growth later. It is one of those cycles of creation that God put in place.

The death that came into creation written about in Genesis chapter three is called the fall. God initiated the redemption plan on the mulch of that fall. He still does. His redemptive plan is like His nature, unchanging. He can bring new life from desperate situations. In His creative and redemptive work, there is hope for life emerging from a fallen world as Jesus is lived (Phil. 1:21) and proclaimed.

There is also the fertilized seedbed for the Word of God to produce growth when the heart dies to self and falls into the recognition of need. That kind of hungry heart is compared to good soil in the Bible. "But the one who received the seed that fell on good soil is the man who hears the word and understands it. He produces a crop, yielding a hundred, sixty or thirty times what was sown" (Matt. 13:23).

Some things God rakes away and removes, other things He redeems and transforms. He can grow seeds of new life on the seedbed of compost discarded. When confession and repentance happen, it is not unlike the autumn leaves being shed. When we count ourselves dead to sin (Rom. 6:11), the world can see creative new colors.

New life also comes forth on the soil of good things dropped for better things. God can grow a crop yielding more than what was sown on the soil of an obedient heart. That is something to celebrate, and it makes my heart sing as I enjoy the colors of autumn.

Winter's Cross

Winter seems like a powerful illustration of death, with leaves gone from the trees and cold temperatures that stop growth. The wintry death, however, contains the seeds of new life. Green sprouts bud forth each spring. The cross is a profound image of cold death that brings forth new life. Wooden beams were fashioned from a green tree that was killed, and Jesus died upon it. But the spring of resurrection life is also truth. The cross cannot be separated from the Resurrection. The cross, like winter, has a purifying effect.

I remember when we moved to Fortine, Montana, and enjoyed our first winter in the mountainous area. Our elderly neighbor grabbed my arm one day and invited me over to an open field next to her house with the invitation, "Come look at this."   As I looked curiously up on the mountainside at the fresh snow, I admired the wonderful view that the mountains provide with that first snowfall gently salting the hills. I commented about the beauty of the green pine and fir trees being blanketed with light snow, thinking that was what she wanted me to see. She challenged me, "Look closer."

As I gazed at the mountain, wondering what she was referring to, a wonderful image suddenly took shape before my focusing eyes. The perfect shape of a cross was formed by a gap in the trees and terrain near the top.   It was marvelous. I was inspired and we shared a moment of quiet worship together.

The principle of the cross can be seen all over the created order. It is a principle that every follower of Jesus lives.   Seasons that feel like death in the wilderness lead to deeper places of new and transformed life in Christ, the hope of glory. As Paul wrote in his epistle to the Corinthian church:

> We always carry around in our body the death of Jesus, so that the life of Jesus may also be revealed in our body. For we who are alive are always being given over to death for Jesus' sake, so that his life may be revealed in our mortal body (2 Cor. 4:10-12).

Counting the Cross

Sometimes great lessons from the Bible are put in the negative. For example, what are the consequences of *not* taking up my cross to follow Him? Jesus said it this way, "And anyone who does not carry his cross and follow me cannot be my disciple" (Luke 14:27). In that passage, Jesus goes on to talk about counting the cost. He summarizes later in the passage, "In the same way, any of you who does not give up everything he has cannot be my disciple" (Luke 14:33). These are powerful and convicting words about the negative of hanging onto *things* at the expense of experiencing the life-giving embrace of Jesus. I cannot be His disciple if I am bound to this world and wrapped up in deadly, consuming self interest. That includes an attitude of apathy about creation or selfish abuse of the environment and its resources.

A friend of ours had a flooded basement due to a plumbing problem. I was impressed with her attitude. She simply cleaned up and moved on, without a consuming care about the *things* which may have been lost in the dirty waters. She is a person in love with Jesus and not burdened by unhealthy attachments to possessions that could hold her back from being a devoted disciple of Christ. She has experienced His cleansing, living waters of life.

At the cross of Christ was suffering and rejection. That is the cost, rejecting all else, even to the point of sharing in His sufferings (even in flooded basements of life), in order to gain Christ. As in the words of Scripture:

> But whatever was to my profit I now consider loss for the sake of Christ. What is more, I consider everything a loss compared to the surpassing greatness of knowing Christ Jesus my Lord, for whose sake I have lost all things. I consider them rubbish, that I may gain Christ (Phil. 3:7-8).

As Dietrich Bonhoeffer put it in his classic, *The Cost of Discipleship:*

> The cross is laid on every Christian. The first Christ-suffering which every man must experience is the call to abandon the attachments of this world. It is that dying of the old man which is the result of his encounter with Christ. As we embark upon discipleship we surrender ourselves to Christ in union with his death----we give over our lives to death. Thus it begins; the cross is not the terrible end to an otherwise god-fearing and happy life, but it meets us at the beginning of our communion with Christ.[33]

Does this kind of thinking not promote the sacrifice that can flow into stewardship as an act of worship to the God who creates, redeems, transforms, and restores? There are many ways that Jesus followers will be called to count the cost and live with intentional sacrifice. The stewardship of creation care is one of those ways.

Cross Loads

Does the magnitude of need in terms of environmental concern seem overwhelming? Is the immensity of the problem part of the reason for apathy and lack of concern? We can't do everything, but we can do something.

Our oldest son had very large blisters on his hands from rope burns he incurred during a rappelling expedition. He found it difficult to achieve some aspects of the work before him because of the wounds. When I asked him what he had learned, he said, "Smaller cliff, thicker gloves."

I believe that is God's offer to us, smaller cliffs and thicker gloves, along with the solid lifeline of His grace. Jesus said it this way, "Take my yoke upon you and learn from me, for I am gentle and humble in heart, and you will find rest for your souls. For my yoke is easy and my burden is light" (Matt.11:29-30). We may get blisters working the garden and stewarding the forest. The work is hard, but being in a relationship with Jesus is what puts the heart at ease. We will face hardship and suffering, but walking with Jesus lightens the burden. His work is easier when it is His work from His hands in His favor and in His strength.

Those hard-working hands of Jesus, who had labored as a carpenter, were nailed to beams of wood. He died on rugged lumber in order to set my hands free to work with that which He puts before me. He gives me the blessing of work, out of the comforting shadow of His favor, a shadow cast by that old rugged cross.

He who was and is the Master Carpenter gives us the blessing of a life-building work in the shadow of His favor. However, I'm not called to sleep in that resting favor. As A.B. Simpson put it:

> One of the greatest enemies to faith is indolence. It is much easier to lie and suffer than to rise and overcome. It is much easier to go to sleep on a snow bank and never wake again than to rouse one's self and shake off the lethargy and overcome the stupor. Faith is an energetic art. Prayer is intense labor. The effectual working prayer of the righteous man availeth much. Satan tries to put us to sleep as he did the disciples in the garden.[34]

Consider the closing verse of Psalm 90, "May the favor of the Lord our God rest upon us; establish the work of our hands for us---- yes, establish the work of our hands."   Get your hands green in the shadow of what He accomplished to set your hands free (Psalm 90:17). Use your hands not simply for natural environmental concern but for supernatural creation care.

The Cross and the Resurrection

I heard an inspiring children's story once about a caterpillar who fell in love. Charley caterpillar fell in love with Amanda caterpillar. They dreamed and planned their life together, which included climbing the big vine that rose to the heavens. Thousands of caterpillars had gone before them, climbing and ascending to disappear into the sky toward some glorious pinnacle of success.

Finally, their day came. They began the assent together.   They climbed and climbed, making progress as a team. After awhile, they noticed that they were crawling over the aging bodies of relatives fused to the vine who were no longer able to make the climb. Yet upward they continued, pushing on in the face of death.

Eventually, they realized that only one of them would be able to make it to the top. Both of them were not going to be able to make the final steps. Charley broke Amanda's heart when he pushed off, using her as leverage, to make it the rest of the way. He made the final leap. Amanda was left in the wake of his victory. She climbed back down the vine alone, broken hearted and discouraged.

With his final lunge to the top, Charley expected to see the pinnacle of creation and the ultimate dream come true. He envisioned all goals, hopes, and dreams fulfilled. What he saw was depressing. Amongst the clouds he saw thousands of carcasses of those who had climbed before him, leaping to their deaths when they discovered that there was nothing there. He sat immobilized in the face of empty death. For a long time he reflected on the hopelessness, the broken dreams, and the love he had left behind.

From below suddenly emerged a beautiful winged creature, colorful and graceful, beckoning him to follow. That he did.   He descended back down the vine, all the way to the bottom and over to an empty shell of a cocoon. It was then he recognized the butterfly as

Amanda, transformed yet familiar. He discovered the truth of the cocoon which leads to a beautiful life.

I like that story. The butterfly displays a marvelous example in creation of the beautiful life cycles which include a season of death-like circumstances. Butterflies emerge from a tomb-like place of confinement transformed. Each stage of life is only achieved through struggle, and each is necessary to become fully grown. It involves change. A personal application is appropriate. As A.B. Simpson said it, "God loves to take the things in our own lives that have been the worst, the ardest and the most hostile to God, and transform them so that we shall be the opposites of our former selves."

The caterpillar spins silk that becomes a cocoon, later to break free to be what the Creator made it to be. The story and the reality of something beautiful coming forth from ugly wrappings is packed within the shadow of the cross and the resurrected life.

Death Brings Life

The principle of death bringing forth life is a message of the cross that can be seen in illustrative ways in creation around us. We spent several days at my parents' home one summer, helping with some projects. One of the chores was to clean out the rain gutters. The main drain on one side of the house was completely clogged. Upon closer inspection, we discovered the reason it was plugged. Something had gotten stuck in one of the corners of the gutter drain, and leafy materials had accumulated there. An acorn found itself stuck in that spot as well. The seed must have, in essence, died right there. That's what seeds do, die to bring forth new life.

So, the acorn grew into a small oak tree out of that place of death. Its roots had spread out for nutrition and it sprouted right out through the joint.   There it was, growing out of the corner of the drain up near the roof. I was amazed, and also enjoyed some quiet reflection on an inspiring green creation lesson.

I wish I had taken a picture. It would be fun to play with potential captions:

- *When you feel stuck, let God bring forth new life*
- *You can fight or switch....to God's marvelous life-giving possibilities*

- *When God blesses you with the opportunity to die to yourself at a corner in life, embrace the transformation of new life in Christ*
- *Blossom where you are*
- *Grow with renewed life under the hand of God no matter how grim the situation looks*

Life and transformation are not limited by our capacity to find ourselves in a jam or at an inhibiting corner. In fact, marvelous things can happen out of a tough place to the encouragement of others. "He is not the God of the dead, but of the living, for to him all are alive" (Luke 20:38). If we try to get out of a jam God has allowed us to be in, we might be working against Him. Trying to save your life might mean losing it. Losing your life for Jesus brings new life discovery with light and growth in the darkest places (Matt. 16:24-26). That is a wonderful shadow of the cross.

God Creates and Recreates New Life

I love the account in Genesis chapter two of how God took dirt, or dust, and breathed life into that handful of earthy stuff. If I were to blow into a handful of dirt, I'd get nothing but a dirty face. When God created Adam and breathed life into him (Gen. 2:7), He created him with purpose and meaning.

Because of the events of Genesis chapter three, death now reigns in creation. That death is a curse that paralyzes humanity and creation, prohibiting us from really taking care of nature and being good stewards. That death touches every flower, every tree, every blade of grass, and turns God's garden into a wasteland and desert in need of new waters of life.

When Jesus came in the incarnation, went to a cross, and brought forth life in the resurrection, He paved a way for all creatures and creation to be redeemed and restored to the wholeness of the original garden![35] As the Bible puts it, "Therefore, if anyone is in Christ, he is a new creation; the old has gone, the new has come!" (2 Cor. 5:17).

This is more than good theology. It is more than illusive theories or subconscious dreams for building hope. It is real. It is within our reach. To quote Paul once again (maybe you'll have this verse memorized by the end of the book), "For since the creation of the world God's invisible qualities---his eternal power and divine nature---have been clearly seen, being understood from what has been made, so that people are without excuse" (Rom. 1:20). God's nature and His plan are within reach for every person. Because He is a caring Creator revealed in the finely-tuned work of His hands, the gospel is the most believable reality in cosmic history.

The perfect and caring God of the universe who created humans did not exterminate them when they demonstrated imperfection, nor did He simply overlook the injustices and disobedience of the first people. He had a plan. Consider the explanation of Fred Heeren:

> The best option is one we never would have guessed on our own: God offers His creatures a choice to be permanently changed, to become a new creation. The good news involves a just death penalty and a full pardon---perfect justice and unbounded mercy. And He offers us the best possible reason to enter a love relationship, by demonstrating sacrificial love toward us first through Jesus Christ.[36]

Before going to the cross, Jesus prayed in a place called the Garden of Gethsemane. That garden is the garden of reversal. It is new water for the parched ground. It is new blood for the life of the world. For here the new creation begins.[37] The resurrection of Jesus Christ is a second act of creation, a new beginning that will be culminated in His coming again to reestablish the garden, to bring humanity into His own communal life, and to rule over creation forever![38]

Apart from Christ, no human being can restore the beauty of creation as found in the garden. In Christ we can participate with His re-creative work and serve as stewards of all that He has made. When we enter into a relationship with the living Christ, we have the opportunity to be a part of renewing, restoring, and caring for creatures and creation to the eternal glory of God. Whether you believe in a total destruction of the earth for a new heaven and earth or a restored creation from elements in our world today, it does in no way minimize the value of worshipful living through creation care as part of the gospel witness.

Webber, in his book, *Ancient-Future Worship*, makes a

distinction between liberal Christians and conservative Christians in this regard. He suggests that liberal Christians have a creation theology without an incarnation, leading to an emphasis on humanitarian social action at the expense of redemptive social witness that proclaims and lives the gospel. Conservative Christians, on the other hand, have an emphasis on redemption theology which focuses almost entirely on the death of Jesus and therefore ignores the connection between creation, incarnation, and re-creation. The results, according to Webber, are that conservative Christianity concentrates on snatching the soul from the body to save it from an eternity in hell.[39]

Some of what he says rubs me a bit, but that is because I am in the conservative Christian camp. Webber expresses valid concerns. The gospel is about the good news of salvation from an eternity in hell through faith in Jesus Christ. That needs to remain a critical, eternal concern that motivates the passion for reaching out to people in need of redemption. However, that truth does not diminish the need for social justice and caring for all of creation as a way to honor and respect the Creator. There is a place of biblical tension between the extremes. Some would call it a holistic approach.

Living in the shadow of the cross means that the truth about the Bible's teaching on eternity is embraced without avoiding the powerful message of the incarnation of Jesus, His death on the cross to pay the penalty for sin, and the resurrection life that sets people free to live victoriously in this world. Abundant life includes creation care that proclaims the good news message of the cross and the resurrection.

Save the Turtles

Kristi saved a turtle one morning. We were out walking together and there he was, navigating his way across the road. I suppose from his perspective all he could see was the nice paved expanse for easy travel. Perhaps he figured crossing that road was all he needed to accomplish today. It was his most important task and became his goal for life, moving from the manicured lawn on the one side to God's beautiful open creation of rich forest beyond the blacktop path. Maybe a few passing cars set him into panic mode, and there he was in the middle of the pavement of a busy road. Kristi saved his life, picking him up and ushering the turtle into immediate safety. The quick flight may have been terrifying for him, but I'm sure it was redemptive and peaceful to find himself in the safety and beauty of the spacious wooded environment on the other side.

The whole incident reminded me of salvation in Christ. I've been the turtle, sticking my neck out for greener pastures. I spent years trying to cross the road toward God in my own strength. It was, most of the time, the slow and limited perspective of the turtle. I was totally unaware of the dangers around me, vehicles of speedy destruction passing by much too closely. Sometimes I was crippled by fear, retreating into the false security of a fragile shell. I came to understand the impossibility of crossing over by my own efforts and work. I came to understand that hiding beneath thin coverings of self sufficiency or religious garments of protection offered no real peace.

The day I stuck my neck out and trusted Jesus Christ alone was the day of salvation. I called out to Him, and experienced what is expressed in the words of the Bible, "The Lord will hear when I call to Him" (Psalm 4:3b). I experienced His gentle hand. He alone knows how to pick us up and usher us to the safety of the other side. The flight path is sometimes scary, but the safest place to be is in His hands. He sees the bigger picture, the whole road with all of its dangers. He could have looked the other way and left us on our own, but His love is too great.

His forests are rich and beautiful, and He alone can carry us there. Loving submission to Him is the path to deliverance. Living life in the shadow of the cross is the only appropriate response to His salvation. I am a saved turtle who crossed over. I hope you are too.

Shadows of the cross are not always easy to detect or understand, but God is good at opening eyes and ears to see and hear as a blessing of following Jesus. As Paul said it, "The message of the cross is foolishness to those who are perishing, but to us who are being saved it is the power of God" (1 Cor. 1:18).

The cross life is marked by deep, pure joy. "You have filled my heart with greater joy than when their grain and new wine abound. I will lie down and sleep in peace, for you alone, O Lord, make me dwell in safety" (Psalm 4:7-8). That is authentic green.

It is easy to learn the doctrine of personal revival and victorious living; it is quite another thing to take our cross and plod on to the dark and bitter hill of self-renunciation.

~A.W. Tozer~

For Reflection/Discussion:

1. What keeps you from working in the world of creation care?
2. What could you do to your physical environment to have it nurture you, relax you, or empower you?
3. What do you think of Robert Webber's comments (pages 104-105)? In what ways do you agree or disagree?
4. What does it mean to deny yourself and take up your cross to follow Him?
5. Who in your sphere of influence needs to hear the message of the cross?
6. Where have you denied yourself of resources on behalf of another person?
7. Reflect on this anonymous quote, "You don't have to cross the sea to see the cross, but you have to see the cross to cross the sea."

God grades on the cross, not the curve.
~Anonymous~

Chapter 8

The Hunt for Green October

As the deer pants for streams of water,
so my soul pants for you, O God.
~Psalm 42:1~

I am a hunter. I don't believe the Bible condemns it.[40] Jesus fed fish to people and Peter's vision included killing and eating meat (Acts 10:9-13).

October is the month of hunting. One of the things I like about hunting is the chance to enjoy creation and cultivate healthy thoughts about God's beauty. Hunting for me is opportunity for solitude and prayer, with an open Bible when sitting in a tree stand or perched on a log. I have missed chances to put meat in the freezer because I was focused on drinking deeply of a particular passage in the Bible, but the spiritual nourishment was worth it.

One particular year I was hunting elk in Wyoming. Late in the afternoon, after a long day of walking and enjoying the mountains, I sat down on some rocks and took out one of my backpacking Bibles. I started reading John fifteen, where Jesus said, "I am the vine; you are the branches. If a man remains in me and I in him, he will bear much fruit; apart from me you can do nothing" (John 15:5). The Bible I was reading translated the passage a different way. Instead of using the words, "bear much fruit," the word "harvest" was used.

I mulled that over in my mind, having never seen that version of the verse before. Remaining in a relationship with Jesus means you bear fruit. You produce a harvest. As I thought about the connection between a relationship with Jesus and the idea of harvest, I looked up and saw a large bull elk. So, I raised my rifle and harvested him.

I was blessed with the fruit of some really good meat for the freezer that day. It was a good harvest on several levels. Hunting for truth in the Bible always feeds the hungers of the heart. A heart hungry and thirsty for God produces a fruitful harvest.

Shifting Shadows

I remember watching a high elevation Montana meadow where the elk had been feeding. I was reading Psalm nineteen and thinking about how the heavens declare the glory of God. The psalmist wrote that God has pitched a tent for the sun, and it rises in one end of the heavens and makes its circuit to the other. As I reflected on that passage, I took note of how things change as the sun makes its course over a few hours. As the sun moves across the sky, things take on different shapes. The colors shift, shadows disappear in one place and show up in another, and new things appeared as the rays of light set upon them.

Deep in thought, my eyes caught a particular shadow that I hadn't noticed before. I thought to myself, "That shadow by the tree really has the shape of an elk." My eyes focused. It was an elk, looking directly at me. I was already detected and pegged by the large bull, what they call "busted" in the hunting world. My deep reflections on the words of a Psalm and shifting shadows spared the big animal from ending up in my freezer that day.

Prior to becoming a follower of Jesus, hunting was a religious experience for me. There was some primal instinct at play and I loved the world of hunting. Success meant harvesting a trophy deer, elk, bear, large pheasant, or other creature. I always used the meat and had sound hunting ethics, but hunting was a sport that also became an obsession and an expensive pursuit.

When I made a decision to become a true Christian, there was some major shifting that took place in my heart. The light of Jesus shifted some shadows. Deciding to become a Jesus follower didn't cause me to give up hunting. In fact, I think I enjoy it more because of an enlightened viewpoint.

My new attitude could be captured in the actions of a friend I hunted with once. He harvested a bull elk, and the first thing he did as we approached the deceased animal was intriguing to me. He leaned his gun against a tree, took off his hat, got down on one knee, and prayed a wonderful prayer of thanksgiving to the one who created the elk. He thanked God that the animal didn't suffer and that his bullet was true and hit the mark. He expressed gratitude for the meat that would help feed his family and others. It was a beautiful way to show respect for the creature and the Creator who provides.

Why Hunt?

My hunting friends can relate to the pause created by the question, "Why do you hunt?" I like what Todd Tanner said, "We hunt because we have a visceral connection to the land, one we simply can't ignore. A connection, I might add, that stands in stark contrast to the social and cultural insanity that surrounds us."[41] Tanner further develops the notion that the problem can be summed up by the word "consumers." Too many of us accept that label without offense, because that is the reality we live in. It represents a broken bond with the natural world of creation.

In contrast to being a consumer, hunters with integrity realize that the role of being stewards and caretakers identifies an important purpose beyond simply harvesting wildlife and using resources. Hunters do hunt because they love the outdoors, and because they love to eat wild game. They also love the excitement and the challenge. However, these are incomplete answers to the *why* question. As Tanner describes it, these are simply ripples on the pond which can obscure the quiet depths below.

I remember the last time I went elk hunting. When the alarm went off, I didn't want to get up. Staying in that warm bed snuggled up with my wife is where I really wanted to stay. Why in the world would I get out from under the blankets and step out into the cold dark world outside?   There was enough of a breeze blowing that I knew it would be chilling cold. I would face icy fingers, frozen toes, a biting frost on my ears, and the fatigue of trying to carve a path through snow that had fallen the night before.

I got up because I had to. I am a hunter. My hunting friends understand.   The memories, the connections with a wealth of human history marked by hunters, the heritage, the possibilities of building a new memory, the prospect of a new creation lesson, the anticipation of seeing a bull elk or other critter that few humans ever get to lay eyes on; I didn't bother to ask myself why.

True Hunting is Marked by Conscience

I hunt deer and elk for the meat. It is not about a misplaced caveman urge to kill, it is about the thrill of the hunt and the benefit of harvested food. Actually, the wild game is a healthy source of nutrition. I remember one year when we were able to harvest several extra deer, more than we needed, so we looked for people to give the meat to. One particular lady in our church indicated that her doctor had informed her that she could no longer eat beef because of a medical condition she was facing. However, she was encouraged to eat all the wild meat that she wanted. So, we were able to bless her with the gift of some good food.

Hunting just for the sport of it falls short. Some of my hunting buddies might say I've gone "soft" with that statement, but I've discovered a deeper place of joy in the adventure of hunting. I cannot condemn the hunting sport or the industry that feeds it, but there is more. Hunting with integrity and conscience takes a person beyond harvesting game animals. When an animal dies, it is not something to celebrate in a prideful way. It calls for respect and honor for an animal that God created.

It can be considered good stewardship to hunt, but the thrill is not in the killing. Fishing is called fishing, not catching. Hunting is just that, hunting and not killing. The greatest excitement is in the hunt.

My family and I had a great time on an antelope hunt once. I made a *big circle* to look for peripheral deer and antelope to chase to Kristi and our two sons as they sat waiting in a place with a good view. On the way around the forested hills, I managed to sneak up on a deer laying asleep on a ridge. I was able to get so close that I could see her eyelashes. I watched her chest rising and falling in the rhythm of breathing. I just couldn't shoot the creature as it slept there, basking in the afternoon sun. The deer was just too close and personal. Instead, I clapped my hands together and shouted, "Gotcha!" I was so near that I could see her eyes get big just before she bailed off the mountain. LOL (I laughed out loud).

I also remember, when running a trap line as a teenager, that a beautiful red fox crossed in front of me at a dead run. I saw him, but he didn't see me. I managed to remain undetected, frozen in place. I was captivated by his amazing color.

The condition of the fresh snow that day was such that walking without detection presented an opportunity to sneak up on him. So, that I did, with the intent of harvesting him. I knew that his pelt would bring a good price.

I watched carefully as he ran along a fence line, found a place he liked, and laid down for a nap. I decided to see how close I could get to him. Because of the layer of soft snow and the perfect direction of a soft wind, I was able to sneak silently into his world.

As I approached, getting closer and closer, admiring his marvelous bright coat, my goal changed. I got to within ten yards of the beautiful animal. I stood there for awhile, captivated by the sight of the little creature all curled up with his nose tucked into his front legs. I was so close that I could see his whiskers and his lungs going up and down. His fur was so plush and full. I was frozen in time, enjoying the way he was curled up with that bushy tail covering his eyes, providing protection over his head.

Instead of pulling the trigger on my rifle, I pulled a different trigger. Although his fur would have paid well, I decided to surprise him rather than harm him. I slowly tucked my rifle under my arm, clapped my hands as loud as I could, and shouted "BOO!"

I couldn't contain my amusement and broke the silence with laughter as he ran around in a circle and high tailed it for cover, unsure of where the threat was coming from. He ran away along the fence line like a red bullet as the joy welled up within me in the thrill of a rare and amazing moment.

Interrupting his nap in such a way might sound mean, but he went on to live another day and learned a life-preserving lesson. So did I. The original goal was modified and I pulled the trigger in a different way. When we hunt for and aim at something, God might change the goals along the way. He might also change the outcome so that we experience a harvest of a different kind, with more meaningful results.

If I were not a hunter, I would not be carrying those great memories of the fox and the deer. The hunts were fruitful and fun because I went hunting. I also enjoy the thrill of reflecting on the creation lessons of those two delightful experiences.

Can you relate to the fox and the deer? Sometimes the circumstances of the world take us off guard and surprise us. Sometimes we react to life's *gotcha* moments by running in circles, looking comical. I'm continuing to learn the strategic value of resting in Christ, being grounded in Him by being in the right place, rooted in His Word, quickly running to Him and calling out to him in those moments when life surprises me. God is not taken by surprise; He has a plan for us, a plan not to harm us but to give us hope and a future (Jer. 29:11). I hope you can find assurance in that today. Christ can be your anchoring hope. His Word gives insights and warnings that help us not to snooze in the wrong place. Taking a peaceful nap along one of His fence lines is a wonderful, safe place.

Hunters and Anti-Hunters

There are people on both sides of the fence and many in the middle of the hunting issue.   Some people take up a vegetarian diet for reasons that have to do with the subject, while others take up intense arguments with the anti-hunting crowd.

I have no desire to get into the politics, but I would like to suggest that there is a middle ground. Wise hunters are sensitive to the viewpoints of other people. They avoid flaunting their successfully filled tags by driving around with game on their hood. Anti-hunters are wise to study and consider the motives and mindsets of people who love to hunt. Meaningful conversations are possible. There is a common ground in the place of stewardship and creation care that can be embraced by both sides.

Significant advances have been made in the world of game management, helping to keep herds of animals healthy and prevent things like overgrazing and starvation. Some of the most conservation conscious people I know are people who love to hunt and fish.   It could be argued, on a number of levels, that hunting is conservation. Hunters who donate money, pay license fees, and even contribute physical labor for habitat improvement are in the ranks of those who are making a positive impact.

Here is something to consider. What about the aspect of connecting with the historical existence of mankind on earth.   All along, humans have been hunters and gatherers.   It is a history, a heritage, and a source of story.   One of the positive things about the hunting culture is the wealth of stories that can be passed on from one generation to the next.   Hunting stories have components of danger, challenge, adventure, success and failure, and lessons learned to encourage others.

Steve Chapman is a hunter who is also a great story teller. In his book, *A Hunter Sets His Sights*, he talks about the merging of effort and opportunity in the hunting world. He describes it this way:

If you say the words "the moment of truth" to a hunter, more than likely his or her eyes will immediately light up and sparkle with exuberance. Why? Because it describes the thrilling moment when *effort* and *opportunity* converge in the woods or in the field. The *effort* is the work, practice, planning, and strategy a hunter puts into pursuing and outsmarting an elusive creature such as a whitetail deer, bear, elk, or wild turkey. The *opportunity* is the sudden sighting of the game of choice and the nerve-testing realization that it has come close enough to be in range of a shot that might result in taking the trophy home.[42]

People who do not find any pleasure in hunting might argue that the thrill of effort and opportunity could be fulfilled in other ways. However, there is also a heritage involved that is passed from one generation to the next by the telling of stories and the building of new ones.

Success isn't always about taking the trophy home. Sometimes success is the moment when you could take the trophy home. Some of the best hunting stories I have heard and told are about the one that got away. Many of my favorite stories are in that camp. They are fun to tell to younger hunters because it builds their anticipation and feeds a dream that they might be the ones to get a chance at the big animal and build a new memory of their own. I'd love to share some of those stories with you around a campfire sometime.

As the Deer

If I could request a favorite meal, it would be a deer or elk steak covered with mushrooms and onions from the garden fried in a big kettle over the campfire along with some hash brown potatoes. Maybe a side of baked beans would really top that off, but the meat is the treat.

I also hunger in the hunt for lessons of the deer and elk. The psalmist wrote, "As the deer pants for streams of water, so my soul pants for you, O God. My soul thirst for God, for the living God. When can I go and meet with God?" (Psalm 42:1-2). I meet with God every time I am enjoying His creation, and that is worth hungering and hunting for.

Deer often remain in herds with others who know of feeding grounds and safe places. Groups can heighten the awareness of danger. Traveling together, deer stay on the most efficient trails with the least danger. They discover with other deer the best routes to water and green pastures.

I'm told that some bucks stay isolated from the herd during much of the year, and sometimes to their peril. Wolves and other predators are hindered by herds that have more watchful eyes and more awareness of flight avenues. A lone buck can become a target.

Now there is a great lesson from the deer. My thirst grows through fellowship, and so does protection. Christian friends during dry times in rough pastures are like drinks of fresh water for the soul. Safer, greener pastures are discovered in the context of community.

One of the most common sights a deer hunter experiences when searching for a whitetail is just that, a white tail. To humans, the raising of a white flag means surrender. To a deer it means victory. You might think they are high tailing in fear. I think when a deer raises its tail as if to say goodbye, they are really saying "Gotcha, I win." Sometimes white flight is the best option, even a path to victory for humans.

Another fascinating lesson of the deer for me is the way they hurdle obstacles, like fences. Finding a low spot or a loose wire, they make their way over or under the barriers. I love to be around and follow those who hurdle obstacles in their walk of faith.

I also really enjoy hunting antelope, which are similar to deer. Some people call them prairie goats or speed goats. You can see them from miles away. Camouflage is not their defense mechanism. Danger initiates flight with lightning speed. Where did they get their name? Each works like an "ant" to find food in the desert, but their run is not at all limited to a lope. Ante-zoom might be a more appropriate name. Antelope work hard, and that is an example for us. As the proverb says, "Go to the ant you sluggard, consider its ways and be wise" (Prov. 6:6). You can also learn from the antelope.

As I drove across the western plains one day, I pondered some antelope lessons. I want my faith to be seen readily on the open fields of life, yet able and committed to speedy flight when danger and temptations lurk on the horizon. Rather than simply blending in, camouflaged and conformed to the world, a better goal is to be set apart as a vessel being transformed by God. This can happen in a way that compliments the environment.

Antelope stick together. In dry and dusty areas, they can be seen on the horizon, popping their heads up from the security of lush places. They hang out in community, running a shared race, sometimes even playfully. At other times they can be spotted resting in the sagebrush on the hillsides where the sun provides warmth. That is an honorable goal, to bask with others in the SON and run with others in joy.

You can see antelope best when they are moving. That is a good goal, to keep moving forward, pressing on, "…on toward the goal to win the prize for which God has called me heavenward in Christ Jesus" (Phil. 3:14).

I hunt deer and antelope for the harvesting of meat for food. However, I do so with tremendous respect for them. I equally enjoy them and the lessons they can offer.

Green Smells

Does green have a smell? October is certainly characterized by memorable odors for me. One particular year, a good friend sent an extremely memorable box for Christmas. We were serving overseas, in Irian Jaya (West Papua). It was a gift I will never forget. Inside the box was a piece of Montana larch wood, a favorite tree. It smelled of the Rocky Mountains. With the piece of wood was a vial of elk scent. That smell wasn't so pleasant to people around me, but it was precious to me because of the memories of the hunt.

If I were not a hunter, there are smells I would never have smelled. Some were good, some bad, but satisfying because of the associated memories and the stories brought to mind.

One unpleasant smell packed with memories is skunk scent. Somewhere I had read that the only smell successful in hiding human scent is skunk. It might have been a joke, but I became consumed by the idea. I purchased a bottle of the terrible odor and smeared it on one of my special hats to wear when hunting. It became the stinky hat. I got used to it, but my friends never did. And I wondered why nobody was excited about hunting with me during that season. I wonder if a smell that bad is the smell of what happened in Genesis chapter three, the smell of broken relationships.

Some things smell really good. As the wise writer said it, "Perfume and incense bring joy to the heart, and the pleasantness of a friend springs from their heartfelt advice" (Prov. 27:9). In Hebrew poetry, found in Psalms, Proverbs, and elsewhere in Scripture, the characteristic rhythm isn't rhyming words but repetition of thought. Wisdom and truth are often echoed with the same idea using different language or deeper words, the two statements complimenting each other. Such is the case with Proverbs 27:9.

As perfume and incense initiate joy in the spirit, heartfelt advice initiates awareness of the pleasantness of a friend. Heartfelt advice has a wonderful fragrance. The aroma of joy fills the air when friends sharpen each other. "As iron sharpens iron, so one person sharpens another" (Prov.27:17). Iron sharpening iron smells good.

Springtime seems to heighten my joy and gratitude for a sense of smell. What smells good to you? Joy smells good. The pleasantness of a friend smells good, and so does good stewardship of creation.

Some things smell good to us because they are connected with precious memories. For me that list would include the smell of gunpowder and Hoppes #9 (a gun cleaning compound). The sweat of a horse, the musky odor of an elk herd, the sweet scent in a field of mountain flowers, the very gentle breeze created with turning the pages of a Bible, and the aroma of freshly brewed coffee are powerful smells packed with memorable moments. And, yes, skunk scent.

I also treasure the smell of campfires, because it connects me with memories of valuable discussions, precious relationships, and images of past biblical heroes sitting around the fire encouraging each other. Watching the dancing flames and smelling the smoke of a warm fire stirs something deep in the heart.

Many odors remind me of fellowship with others on the hunt for truth and special conversations which included wise counsel. I hope you have people in your life like that, friends who care enough to share life with you. I hope you have friends who spur you on toward greater concern for the environment, God's creation. Godly friends and wise counsel in this way has a pleasing aroma. It smells good.

Hitting the Green Mark

My favorite kind of hunting is archery. There is something about a bow and arrow that connects you with a heritage from ages past. The wonderful mystery of wearing camouflage and blending in with the environment is also a special feature of the bow hunting season. The quiet stalking, the listening and waiting, the close-up encounters with critters of all kinds, and the beautiful time of year in the forest are all part of the annual hunt.

As an archery hunter who is also always looking for lessons, I want the flight path of my life to hit the target. I am hungry for my life to make a purposeful mark. The only way for that to happen is through Christ in me, the hope of glory (Col. 1:27). He is the Prince of Peace, the one who enables me to think and practice rightly.

Bow hunters know that a critical part of the equipment is a set of good arrows with sharpened broadheads. Keeping those arrows sharp and ready is a crucial component of a successful hunt. Learning how to aim well ahead of the season is also a must, developing the ability of concentration and focus for opportunities that will arise.

During my final archery season in Montana, before leaving the state, I slowly and carefully snuck up on a bull elk that was sleeping on a hillside. It took me over an hour to put on the sneak. When I finally got into position, I took the shot. I will never forget the dreaded sound of the arrow as it hit the tree, breaking the silence with the unmistakable sound of a metal object striking wood. Somehow, a pine tree had miraculously grown up in the flight path after I let the arrow go. Okay, that might be a stretch of an excuse, but time froze as I watched the big animal disappear.

Sometimes we can't see the forest for the trees. Sometimes we can't see the trees for the forest. Creation care involves both. We need the big picture of animals in need of our help and stewardship. We need the larger view of amazing creatures that we have opportunity to behold and appreciate. At the same time, there are obstacles and opportunities right in front of us that need our attention and care.

After the pain of watching that bull run away, I remembered that success isn't always in the harvesting of an animal. Success that day was in the lesson it taught me and the wonderful memory of having seen such a beautiful animal so close. Had I not been hunting, I would not have had the opportunity to behold his splendor. I pulled the arrow out of the tree, put it in my quiver with its broken broadhead, and smiled with another great memory and lesson learned.

Later that same day, Kristi joined me for an afternoon hunt. We suddenly found ourselves within range of several elk. I quickly loaded my bow with an arrow and prepared to draw for a second-chance shot. Kristi got my attention and pointed out that the arrow I had chosen was missing the broadhead. It was the same arrow I had shot into a tree earlier in the day. It was an arrow with no point.

We certainly don't want to make the same mistake in life. One of the targets we can hit is creation care. Stewardship practices are the various arrows in our quiver that we can make a point with. The state of the environment is a crucial concern today. Some would say that it is the most important issue of our day, and it is packed with the potential to demonstrate contagious acts of worship to the Creator of our world with each shot we take.

I heard about a hunter who asked God before his hunt to keep his arrow flying true. That prayer was answered in a big way, and he ended up shooting a charging grizzly bear and saving his son's life. What if he had used an arrow without a sharp broadhead or with no point at all?

Thinking rightly about the environment is a great target to aim at. Honoring and worshiping the God of creation is a way to stay sharp and live with a point.

Do not conform any longer to the pattern of this world, but be transformed by the renewing of your mind. Then you will be able to test and approve what God's will is — his good, pleasing and perfect will.
~~Romans 12:2~~

For Reflection/Discussion:

1. How does Romans 12:1-2 encourage you in terms of your involvement with His will in creation care?
2. Whether you are a hunter or not, you are hunting and searching for something. Where and how does that show up for you? What are you hunting for?
3. Talk about a time when you got off track in your search and hunt for the wrong thing(s). How did God bring you back?
4. What footprints are you leaving for those coming behind you?
5. There are ranches in Texas and other places that raise exotic animals for hunters to shoot. Some of those animals are endangered or extinct elsewhere, so owners argue that they are doing something good in preserving various species. Some anti-hunting groups argue that it is immoral to raise animals to be shot. What are the pros and cons of these kinds of ranches? How do you feel about it?
6. Are you for hunting or against it? How can you make sure you are keeping bridges open to people on the other side of the issues who might have a different viewpoint?
7. What might you do today to sharpen your involvement in creation care?

Chapter 9

Winged for Conservation Care

If I rise on the wings of the dawn,
if I settle on the far side of the sea, even there
your hand will guide me, your right hand will hold me fast.
~Ps 139:9-10~

Some birds are so intent on equipping their chicks to fly that they actually push them out of the nest when the time is right.   Imagine being the last chick, watching mom push out the first, then the second, knowing that your time is coming. What fears would emerge, being unable to see what is going on below the green branches?   You might decide to hang on for life, even battling in every way the fate ahead.

The mother bird knows what the chick does not. Birds were made to fly. They were created for it. What a shame it would be if they never lived out that delightful capacity to soar above the earth.

In terms of caring for God's creation as a way to worship Him as Creator, it is encouraging to know that He wired us for it. He empowers us to soar with an effective flight path in caring for creation well. Wherever you are on issues regarding the environment and creation care, God's concern exceeds yours. Wherever you are, He is there to help you rise and be empowered by His guiding hand.

We are made for creation care and empowered to do it. It is how we fly. When you don't feel capable of flight, you can be a branch to launch others. A growing relationship with Jesus as Creator, Savior, and Lord enables you to flourish like a palm tree (Psalm 92:12). The older you get, the greener you can be.   "They will still bear fruit in old age, they will stay fresh and green…." (Psalm 92:14).

After God created the first people, He told them to be fruitful, to increase in number, and to fill the earth and rule it (Gen. 1:28). With that command He also reminded them of His provision. "To all the beasts of the earth and all the birds of the air and all the creatures that move on the ground---everything has the breath of life in it---I give every green plant for food" (Gen. 1:28-30). God provides what we need in order to get it done. It was God who created and God who provided. God gave the first humans a command and provided the resources for them to live it out with success. God still empowers us and provides for us to accomplish all that He invites us to do. That includes empowerment for creation care and faithful stewardship.

Built for It

I would not suggest churches get politically involved, but individual followers of Jesus should. It is a right, privilege, and duty as part of witness in and to the world. For sure, people opposed to the Christian faith should not be the primary spokespersons for a biblical cause that is so rooted in the very heart of the Creator. I am convinced that creation care is God's will, and His followers should be the primary agents of reconciliation of people with their Creator, people with people, and people with the created world around them. It is an overflow of worship. People in love with God the Creator have the deepest motive to love nature with genuine concern for the creation, founded in biblical truth. We were built for it.

You can be part of the solution for the problems of a groaning creation. There are many ways in which we can participate in creation care and make a significant, contagious impact. In the Dominican Republic, there is a factory that makes sandals out of discarded automobile tires.[43] What about the Amish culture of Pennsylvania who believe that chemicals poison the ground and that the earth must be treated with some degree of reverence? What about the growing number of farmers who practice reduced impact conservation methods?

What about using discarded materials for works of art? We went with friends to an enormous craft show. It was amazing to experience all the creativity. Some of the crafts were remarkable demonstrations of taking "junk" and turning it into beautiful things.

Things that some people had probably thrown away were picked up and made into something useful and attractive. Jesus is the ultimate example of that kind of creativity. He is really good at making beautiful things out of junk, and He may want to use your hands.

As we walked around Times Square in New York City on vacation, we heard the beautiful sound of a gifted percussionist somewhere in the crowd ahead. We were inspired to march forward toward the increasingly bright tempo. As we drew near, I expected to see a man on a full drum set skillfully making the beautiful beat. As the scene came into view, I was amazed when I observed a man sitting along the sidewalk playing not on drums but on improvised instruments. There were several different sizes of old buckets and containers. Things that would have been perceived as trash items to some people were being used to make a beautiful sound.

God redeems and He creates. He even redeems trash from the past. Some things should remain buried in the dump, but other elements of your past life can be redeemed for ministry to others. God can illustrate redemption in very creative ways.

Regarding creation care, He creates us with the amazing ability to be creative. We are not all artists, but even scientific types are creative in their contributions. He can use our hands to redeem junk and make it something beautiful to the praise of His glory. So be creative. Make a song to the glory of God. Let everything in your reach be used for the praise of our King. As the Bible writer put it, "Praise him with the clash of cymbals, praise him with resounding cymbals. Let everything that has breath praise the Lord. Praise the Lord" (Psalm 150:5-6).

Creation Care Lifts the Heart

I heard a fable once about the way flying creatures first received their wings. As the story goes, God initially made birds without wings. Then He made the wings, set them down before the wingless birds, and said, "Take up these burdens and carry them."

As one writer described the story:

> The birds had sweet voices for singing, and lovely feathers that glistened in the sunshine, but they could not soar in the air.

When asked to pick up the burdens that lay at their feet, they hesitated at first. Yet soon they obeyed, picked up the wings with their beaks, and set them on their shoulders to carry them. For a short time the load seemed heavy and difficult to bear, but soon, as they continued to carry the burdens and to fold the wings over their hearts, the wings grew attached to their little bodies. They quickly discovered how to use them and were lifted by the wings high into the air. The weights had become wings.[44]

One of the weights we carry, if we are paying attention to contemporary issues of environmental concern, is creation care. We need to embrace it as one of the most crucial concerns of the current age. Stewardship just might be one of the wings God desires you to take up. Soar. Clearly, there is a green wind blowing.

I remember enjoying the wind at the beach one day. The wind creates great waves. It was a thrill to watch it do what it does so well, filling sails and enabling kites to fly. I thought about the kite, which does what it does best not just in spite of the wind, but because of it.

The kite has freedom to fly so well because of a thin string in a grounded hand. Slavery to the string sets it free. True freedom is slavery to that which sets a person free. In a similar way, being a slave to Christ as the one who created you and died for you is what sets you free.[45] Grounded in Him by even a thin faith, flying with the wings of the Eagle, even through stormy days of life, is abundant living enabling us to soar.

Bible based creation care is one of the strings that God gives us to stay connected to His guiding hand. Faith flight that values what God can teach about Himself in nature is contagious. You can help others to capture the delight of enjoying the God who made such beauty around us.

I am inspired by the thoughts of Bertha Calloway. She said that we cannot direct the wind, but we can adjust the sails. We were built to worship. We are empowered for it. Worship doesn't just mean singing songs. It includes caring about and learning from the created order. Even in the world of science, the God of creation can be honored by the things that are developed and put to effective use for the benefit of people. On windy days and creation storms, set your sails and see what God wants to teach you.

Biomimicry

How arrogant it is to think that if something is superior in quality and design that we did it. God created a universe with untold complexities and powerful systems of design that declare *His* glory. He has also created us with a unique ability to learn from His design with humility and teachability.

There is a fascinating science called biomimicry that involves innovation of new products using clues and ideas from nature. It is fascinating the way God designed creation. There are untapped resources for designers and engineers to innovate and inspire all of us. God gave humans the intelligence to do more than learn about His creation. He has given us the ability to learn not just about creation but to learn from it. Learning from creation is deeper than simply learning about the environment.

He created us with the ability to initiate practical applications and be innovative, even entrepreneurial with creative design using ideas gleaned from nature. Biomimicry has impacted computer software, water purification processes, engineering, and on and on with more to come. Janine Benyus, in a TED talk,[46] suggested three important questions to address which will add to the world of innovation. First, how does nature make things? In other words, self assembly in things like seashells is a fascinating study that will contribute to the world of crystallization and design.

A second question that she asks is, "How does life make the most of things?" What does the created world teach us about the power of shape, like birds that can dive into the ocean without a splash in order to see fish? Then there is the realm of what we can learn about how creative design enables the quenching of thirst to happen with water. Water is a significant resource in the world, involving challenges of availability. From creation we can learn how to get metals without mining by using water, how animals have adapted and become resilient, how healing takes place, the mechanics of solar transformation, and the list continues to grow.

The third question Janine poses is, "How does life make "things" disappear into systems?" CO_2 for example, is something we normally see as a poisonous problem. That is not so in the created order. Dealing with waste, disposal, stopping chain reactions of certain chemicals, and natural recycling are all issues to which the field of biomimicry can speak.

Did you know that swimsuits have been developed based on the structure of a shark's skin? The skin of a shark is made up of countless overlapping scales with grooves running down their length in alignment with water flow. This design helps water pass by faster, enabling the shark to swim more efficiently.[47] The rough shape also prevents parasitic growth like algae and barnacles. Replicating this design for swimsuits and also the bottom of boats has been an innovative way to learn from creation. God gives us the ability to capitalize on designs and features found in nature.

Velcro is a widely known example of biomimicry. It was invented by Swiss engineer George de Mestral in 1941 after he removed burrs from his dog and studied them to see how they work.[48]

The design of a whale's tail, components of paint, and the shape of birds are among the many ways that people have learned from creation. There are even groups who have suggested organizing the flight path of airplanes in order to travel in teams, utilizing the V-shape of flight as demonstrated by flocks of geese and other birds. It is said that birds using a V-formation are able to boost the distance they are able to fly by more than seventy percent. Researchers at Stanford University suggest that planes taking turns in front as birds do could use fifteen percent less fuel compared to flying solo.[49]

There is a fascinating website, www.asknature.org, which is being used by many people. Green entrepreneurs, innovators, and engineers of various professions are actively engaged in this field of biomimicry and beyond.[50] There is much to be learned from God's creative design in nature all around us. God created us with the ability to be creative and innovative. When we contribute to the world by exercising the wings of creativity and engineering skill, we have opportunity to honor God.

God has a purpose and a plan. He didn't just decide one day to have some creative fun when He put everything in place. He lifts our hearts with the display of His glory. His plan to have His glory displayed and declared is a purpose which includes you. You are winged to be an instrument of praise, declaring His marvelous worth to those who need to know of His majesty.

God's Creation Plan

Jesus cared about and appreciated creation when He walked the earth. One day He said to His followers, "And why do you worry about clothes? See how the lilies of the field grow. They do not labor or spin. Yet I tell you that not even Solomon in all his splendor was dressed like one of these" (Matt. 6:28-29). His care for us means we don't need to worry, we are a part of His plan. He points to the beauty of creation to make His point. We can trust Him. The creation around us declares His sovereignty, His care, and His glory.

To understand His plan and purpose in the heavens declaring His glory is to tap into His wisdom. As John Ray penned it:

> How curiously clothed and adorned with the grateful verdure of herbs and stately trees, either dispersed and scattered singly, or as it were assembled in woods and groves, and all these beautified and illustrated with elegant flowers and fruits.....this also shows forth to them that consider it, both the power and wisdom of God: So that we may conclude with Solomon, Proverbs 3:19, "The Lord by wisdom hath founded the earth, by understanding that he established the heavens."[51]

To experience that kind of wisdom is to grasp God's elevated perspective on the world and apply it to our situations. We flew over the Grand Canyon once. It was wonderful to get the bigger picture of an elevated, distant view. We were able to capture the whole panorama from the canyon source toward the distant destination on the horizon.

It was an amazing scene, but the geographical wonder didn't really look like that much from thousands of feet looking down from above. It was an overview of something we know as magnificent put into perspective. God is the God of magnificence. He is the One who creates and sees it all, all at once.

I would love to walk in the Grand Canyon now, as a way to experience it after seeing it from above. Close inspection, at ground level, would deepen the experience within the context of wisdom. Getting the whole context of depth and width and majesty would be sharpened by having seen a bigger perspective. The grand phenomenon declares the very grand character of God.

To really see the Grand Canyon in this way, from a distance and up close, is to be reminded that something profound happened. To view it from both perspectives brings together the marvels of creation and the perspective of an impressive Creator. He is both sovereign and above all, yet intimately present with us as we walk through life carving out a path that makes a contribution and reveals His higher view.

False religions and cults can separate the Creator above from the Redeemer who came to walk among us to bring opportunity for life through the cross and the resurrection. According to biblical truth, the Redeemer, Jesus Christ, was both the instrument of creation and the redeemer of it. He created and He saves His creation. Any other belief system falls short of truth and reality.

To access God's wisdom is to be blessed by His perspective, applying it within His redemptive plan for the world and the people around us. To embrace green thinking and green people is to be a part of God's reconciling work in restoring creation. It also means rubbing against mistaken philosophies of our day, carving truth into the bedrock of various systems of belief.

Ancient Gnosticism and New Age spirituality, for example, present life as an escape rather than a call to live in this world as a participant in God's redemptive plan for creation. Following Jesus doesn't mean separating creation from redemption or the Creator from the Redeemer. There is only one God who both created and redeems His creation. So, when the Psalmist wrote that the heavens declare the glory of God and the skies proclaim the work of His hands, it includes both creation and redemption. Both the work of creation and the work of the cross come together in Christ.

Christians care about people being recreated in Christ for eternal life, experiencing a redemptive future. Therefore, we should build bridges to those in the world of green in a way that moves beyond this world and into the next. We need to embrace the depth of the truth found in the incarnation of Jesus Christ. As Webber articulated so well:

> "God in the womb of the Virgin Mary united with his entire creation in order to reverse the fallenness of creature and creation by taking into his own body the consequence of sin, which is death. Jesus, as the second Adam, defeated all sin and death that

originated with the first Adam. Just as the first Adam affects all creation because of his sin, so also the second Adam rescues all creation because of His righteousness. In death Jesus defeats death. In his resurrection he begins a new act of creation that will ultimately be fulfilled in his second coming."[52]

Now that is solid truth revealing God's creation plan, declaring the glory of the God who created the sky and everything beneath it and beyond. That includes grand canyons and the heavens above revealing heavenly grandeur, even as reflected on the wings and faces of those who love Him.

Wings of Color

I was sitting under an old apple tree waiting for some deer to come by one warm fall day, trying to memorize some Bible verses from the book of Titus:

> For the grace of God that brings salvation has appeared to all men. It teaches us to say 'No' to ungodliness and worldly passions, and to live self-controlled, upright and godly lives in this present age, while we wait for the blessed hope — the glorious appearing of our great God and Savior, Jesus Christ, who gave himself for us to redeem us from all wickedness and to purify for himself a people that are his very own, eager to do what is good (Titus 2:11-14).

In the midst of that great time with God in His Word, a gorgeous butterfly landed on my leg for a visit. It was a blessing to have his friendship for a few moments. His presence spurred me on to deeper reflection in this Titus passage, thinking about the mysterious themes of grace, salvation, self-control, and godly living in an unfriendly and dangerous world. The words in Titus, along with the timely butterfly, were a snapshot of pure beauty.

The splendor of the butterfly reminded me of God's fingerprints in nature. His bright wings caused me to reflect on the many colors of God's grace among the tribes, tongues, and peoples of the world.

That butterfly also served as a great image of self control, as mentioned in Titus. He seemed a model of simply being the marvelous creature God made him to be, without effort, resting on my leg. He wasn't trying to be peacefully beautiful, he just was. Is there a lesson there for us? Perhaps it is less about working to be godly in a religious artificial sense and more about being what God wants us to be. Maybe it is more about submission to the shaping hands of the Father as He makes us more like Jesus, more beautiful in Him (Rom. 8:28-29).

What if the *being* of my inner life was so immersed in Christ that doing good just happened, like the effortless unfolding of butterfly wings? What a wonderful parallel of loveliness, doing what is good, just being who God made us to be, reflecting His glory. That is a picture of pure beauty. Perhaps God desires to help you unfold your colorful wings to do good in His creation.

At Faith Academy in the Philippines, I was in the middle school office and noticed one of the teachers chasing a butterfly down the hall. She was committed to getting that beautiful creature through a doorway to the glorious sunshine outside, where it could freely live as God designed. Sometimes she chased, sometimes she closed doors, sometimes she whisked air with a broom in the appropriate direction, and sometimes she just stood back to let it fly.

Do you have kids? Remember the goal is to set them free to fly as God designed. Help them break out of the cocoons and emerge toward freedom in Christ. Sometimes you lead and coax, sometimes you chase, sometimes you close doors and distract from the wrong way, and most often you breathe forth prayers on their behalf in the appropriate direction, knowing that your help and theirs comes from God. It would be wise to include helping them to be a generation that learns the value of God's creation.

Green Prayer

I love the prayer in the forth chapter of Acts, "Sovereign Lord," they said, "You made the heaven and the earth and the sea and everything in them….." (Acts 4:24b). You could call that a *green prayer*, a prayer of declaration of who God is and what He has done in creation. It matches the pattern Jesus teaches us to pray in Matthew 6:9, "Our Father in heaven, hallowed by your name."

That prayer we call the Lord's prayer in Matthew chapter six is a powerful pattern for prayer. It begins with honoring and exalting God. The next portion of the prayer also informs us about praying for His kingdom to come and His will to be done on earth as it is in heaven (Matt. 6:10). Followers of Jesus in the church, the community of faith, are to be the tangible expressions of God's kingdom.   One of the ways we can live out kingdom principles and do His will on earth is to love what He loves and care about what He cares about.   I hope by now you are convinced that creation care is a part of that. Maybe, for you, that starts with prayer.

We were sharing in a great time of prayer with good friends one day, on their outside deck, with the afternoon sun contributing warmth and brightening the day. As we prayed, we could hear the dripping water from the melting snow. The cold was being replaced by a new season. The ice was melting away, winter silence interrupted once again by the sights and sounds of new life.

I love that about prayer. A quiet time with God is an intimate, face-to-face, heart-to-heart relational connection with God through the Son, Jesus Christ. It's a time for the Word of God to speak warmth into the heart. It's a time for God to thaw the cold places of our souls.   Prayer tends to melt snow from the mountains of challenge, ushering forth living water that wells up unto eternal life (John 7:38).   Time with God is like pure, fresh, living water rushing down a slope. May the mountains melt before you and may His living water refresh you, and those around you.   As the Bible says it, "The heavens proclaim his righteousness, and all the peoples see his glory" (Psalm 97:5-6). Fly beyond in that truth.

Never confuse motion with action.
~Ernest Hemingway~

For Reflection/Discussion:

1. Discuss the above quote by Earnest Hemingway. In what way are you moving more in the direction of creation care? What actions are you taking that show you care about the nature and the environment?
2. Have you ever been surprised by how easy it is to live without something you gave up or gave away?
3. Consider the science of biomimicry. Do your own study on a plant or animal and ask God to open your eyes to a lesson. Consider the aerodynamics of a flying squirrel, the amazing abilities of an ant, or the silk weaving skills of a spider. Share your thoughts with someone.
4. Write a *green prayer* using one of the psalms or the pattern of Matthew 6:9-13. Include praying for the colorful people around you.
5. What "junk" from your past has God turned into something useful and beautiful? Or, how might you invite Him to do so?
6. What are you afraid to do that would bring God honor and glory if you did it?
7. Read Psalm 139:9-10. How is God guiding you and holding you these days?

Chapter 10

Holding All Things Together

If I see God in everything, He will calm and color everything I see.
~L.B. Cowman~

Jesus Christ holds it all together. Talking about Jesus, the Bible proclaims, "For by him all things were created: things in heaven and on earth, visible and invisible, whether thrones or powers or rulers or authorities; all things were created by him and for him. He is before all things, and in him all things hold together" (Col. 1:16-17).

I carry vivid memories of a particular day when we were serving as dorm parents at a school for missionary children in the Philippines. I woke up a bit drained from a very busy weekend. It was hot. The air was thick, warning that it was going to be an uncomfortable, hot, and humid morning. I anticipated that feeling of being in a sauna after even a short period outside.

One of the kids was late getting up and I was trying not to become frustrated. The new computer had quit working and I had to carve out some time to get it fixed. That would mean several hours in Manila traffic to get it into the hands of computer technicians. With congested traffic, you can eat a meal and read a chapter in a book while waiting at some of Manila's stoplights.

The traffic was horrendous getting the first load of kids to school. I came home to the dorm to find out our yard man had quit so he could move into the city, meaning I'd have to do some of the work by myself. A school vehicle pulled up to the dorm and died, so we pushed it into the yard, the strain felt with some sore muscles. Then the ping pong table fell over onto my ankle. I had a headache. Sweat was dripping down the back of my shirt indicating that it was getting hotter. Then the belt holding my pants together broke. It was symbolic. It's how I felt, like everything was falling apart.

I looked down at my broken belt, ready to strike a wall or something as the frustration rose to a boiling point. Kristi walked into the room, looked at me and the condition of my pants, and started laughing. Then one of the kids came up and gave me an irresistible smile that brightened things up. A tropical butterfly flashed its wings and unfolded some beautiful color. I noticed how blue the sky was. God pulled me back together in a moment of bonded faith. The beauty of people and of creation can be His tools for that.

I thought about the belt of truth that is God's Word (Eph. 6:14), holding things together. I thanked God that kids are fun, and that a loving spouse helps me maintain a sense of humor. God is good at holding all of it together, and sometimes He even uses laughter and joy as the glue. Helping us to enjoy creation is one of the instruments in His arsenal of hope.

Faith Bonds

Faith is being sure of what we hope for and certain of what we do not see (Heb. 11:1). Walking by faith requires something more than a happy face façade. Staying afloat in this world requires standing on the strong substance of foundations unseen.

As Kristi and I walked along the river one day, we observed a flock of ducks that seemed to be standing all in a row on top of the water. It was a humorous and yet curious scene, the water lapping around their firmly planted legs out in the river, a good distance from safe shores. By all appearances they were just happily standing on top of the flowing water.

As we looked more closely, we could see that there was a log submerged just below the surface. It was hidden, unseen to the inattentive eye, not obvious, yet providing solid footing for the ducks. They looked quite content, safe, and happy with their feet planted on a place of refuge. They had all their ducks in a row.

We need to see below the surface of things (2 Cor. 10:7ff), lest we fall and sink. Christ is the solid foundation enabling us to stand. We have the resource of putting our hope in the Word of God (Psalm 119), hidden in the depths of our hearts, below the surface, always ready to steady us even when we feel like we're struggling to swim and battling that sinking feeling. Peter, who walked on the water toward Jesus one day, understood this very well. He wrote, "I have written to you briefly, encouraging you and testifying that this is the true grace of God.   Stand fast in it" (1 Peter 5:12).

Peter is the one who walked on the surface of a lake and stood through stormy seas. He understood the manifest presence and power of Jesus. He came to understand that faith is a deep, sustaining influence beneath the surface which is stabilized by the hand of God. Consider the words of the Psalmist, "He lifted me out of the slimy pit, out of the mud and mire; he set my feet on a rock and gave me a firm place to stand" (Psalm 40:2). Faith binds us together in Him on firm foundations. Creation care through acts of faith enable you to be a faithful participant in God's sustaining work. Beyond green is possible because there are motives of faith beneath.

God Holds People

After pitching our tents at a high elevation lake in the Trinity Alps, we enjoyed the wonder of a magnificent body of water surrounded on three sides by fabulous granite peaks. It reminded me of the Psalm, "As the mountains surround Jerusalem, so the Lord surrounds his people both now and forevermore" (Psalm 125:2). We had some great discussions and prayers around the campfire, enjoying a deep sense that God was there with us, in the midst of mountains that served like sentinels guarding a beautiful place of peace.

The weekend was a great visual aid for me, a reminder that He is my refuge, a strong tower against enemies. It sparked a desire in me to contribute to the beauty somehow. That place was like a creation temple declaring the glory of God. I thought about the words in the Bible:

"With all my resources I have provided for the temple of my God — gold for the gold work, silver for the silver, bronze for the bronze, iron for the iron and wood for the wood, as well as onyx for the settings, turquoise, stones of various colors, and all kinds of fine stone and marble….." (1 Chron. 29:2).

I really like the phrase in that passage, "stones of various colors." We are. "You also, like living stones, are being built into a spiritual house to be a holy priesthood…." (1 Peter 2:5). My conviction is that a part of this priesthood of believers in Jesus means reclaiming our place at the center of human creativity by participating in the beautiful colors of creation care.

On another occasion I was out for a walk and enjoying the beautiful fall colors on the trees. I expressed thanks for the various colors of living stones in our church and in our lives. The hillsides were such a wondrous panorama of color, reds and yellows mixed with orange and gold, accented by shades of green. The scene created a party of praise and worship for my eyes. All the distinct colors standing together were like a picture of unity with diversity. "How good and pleasant it is when brothers live together in unity!" (Psalm 133:1).

The colors together on a hillside sing the glory of God, and so do we. I pray that we can live out the truth of Isaiah 60:21b, "They are the plant I have planted, the work of my own hands to show my greatness." Within you is the potential to bloom where you are planted, revealing God's great hands holding you together with other people and all of creation.

Restored Perspective

Encountering God in creation gives us a more realistic and balanced sense of perspective and scale. As David Henderson described so well:

> As you and I walk through our interior worlds, we are giants. Even the shortest among us stretch nearly to the ceiling in most any room we enter, and we dominate our surroundings. Little wonder we wrestle often with pride and self-importance. How can we think of ourselves as the center of the universe when mountain peaks tower over us, when sea worlds sink to depths we can hardly imagine, or the horizon stands at such a distance from us?[53]

The psalm writer put it well, "O Lord, our Lord, how majestic is your name in all the earth! You have set your glory above the heavens" (Psalm 8:1). There is a great response communicated by the psalmist, a reaction that is contagious and inspiring. It is a response of worship that brings things into proper proportion and gives a wise perspective. "When I consider your heavens, the work of your fingers, the moon and the stars, which you have set in place, what is man that you are mindful of him, the son of man that you care for him?" (Psalm 8:3-4). The psalmist writes further about God crowning humans with glory and honor, expressing His special love for us. However, the context clearly sets things in the framework of a creation that declares His majesty.

Capture the wonder and step outside. Enjoy the beauty of a sunset colored by water vapor wrapped in clouds. Take the time to look at the expanse of the skies littered with countless stars hanging in empty space. Think about the earth itself suspended in the universe with the genius design of rotations around the warming sun. Consider the rhythmic impact of ocean waves and the waters teaming with life beyond. Join with Job in the humble reflection, "And these are but the outer fringe of His works" (Job 26:14a).

Creation is about God's work and His sustaining providence. You can be His instrument to restore elements of creation within your sphere of influence as a servant steward. You can be a tool in God's hands to participate in holding things together. So, what can you do?

Reflect

First, be aware of the creation around you. Reflect deeply. Do you realize that quiet reflection in a place of solitude is something that Jesus modeled? Have you considered the benefit of such a spiritual discipline of the faith? Consider some very pointed remarks by Anne Morrow Lindberg:

> The church is still a great centering force for men and women, more needed than ever before---as its increasing membership shows. But are those who attend as ready to give themselves or to receive its message as they used to be? Our daily life does not prepare us for contemplation. How can a single weekly hour of church, helpful as it may be, counteract the many daily hours of distraction that surround it? If we had our contemplative hour at home we might be readier to give ourselves

at church and find ourselves more completely renewed. For the need for renewal is still there.[54]

This was written years ago, but that would not be obvious. Her remarks resonate with a contemporary ring. Reflection focused on Christ out in His creation, sparking moments of worship, is a great way to position yourself to get further direction in accordance with His will. Prayer and solitude is a great place to start making a difference. Appreciation and worship of the Creator in the place of divine reflection can generate creation concern.

To reflect is to realize that nature provides many ethical lessons. Jesus often used nature metaphorically, telling parables to teach spiritual truth. Children of God are compared to sheep that God cares for (Mark 6:34; John 9:36) and Jesus is the good shepherd who brings abundant eternal life (John 10). The Holy Spirit is the water of life (John 4:14). Many parables draw on lessons from seeds, wheat, soil, weeds, rocks, yeast, fish, trees, and fruit to teach about life in the kingdom of God. Lessons abound for the heart that will take time to reflect deeply on created things all around us.

Reduce

Good stewardship as a part of a worship lifestyle means being content with less and resting in the creation of God's provision. It will aid in reducing our impact on the environment. Recycle, reduce, reuse,[55] not out of environmentalist legalism but out of worshipful delight as a child of God free to love and steward what He provides.

This includes refusing to squander or waste resources foolishly. It means sustainable living. It means being less of a consumer and more of a participant to the benefit of people and society. You can make a difference.

Some would call this a life of simplicity. Many Christians would call this a spiritual discipline that goes along with fasting and prayer, including involvement with social justice and ministry to the hurting. If you have never been personally impacted by poverty, a short trip overseas to a third world culture may transform your thinking.

One of the things my family learned by serving overseas is that simplicity can be realized. It is actually amazing what you can live without when you get the opportunity to experience difficult economic times. Why not embrace simplicity as a way to participate in stewardship of creation to the benefit of others?

Resist apathy, reject consumerism, refuse senseless materialism. Learn to be content. Reduce your environmental impact in order to make a higher impact. Other people and the created order will benefit from your sacrifice, and God gets the honor and glory. It also positions you for a greater witness of the good news about Jesus Christ.

Reuse and Recycle

Sadly, we live in a "throw away" world. It is good to adopt a practice of recycling because God put that pattern into the created order. It honors Him to apply those patterns to our own lives. God recycles, and so should we. Consider all the cycles and systems in nature.

The life cycle of a tree is a great example of recycling in creation. Leaves fall, forming leaf litter for nature's recyclers to do their thing. Their work of decomposition breaks down leaf litter into nutrients that will return to the soil and provide what is needed to fertilize and feed trees. New leaves begin the recycling process again.

Creation's recyclers are found in many forms with various jobs in the decomposition recycling process. Bugs, beetles, snails, slugs, worms, and millipedes all have important functions. Fungi, mushrooms, lichens, and microbes of all kinds participate in God's recycling systems, each with a unique role. The next time you have mushrooms on a steak or in a salad, remember that you are eating a recycling agent of God's creation.

If you would like some great ideas of how to be creative and reuse things in your world, attend a few craft shows. Start a process of recycling what you can. Most products these days have markings indicating their recycling capacity. The recycle center is also a great place to meet people and have a conversation about taking care of creation and your own motives for doing so.

Reveal

Nature has intrinsic value because God created, and all created things have worth in His eyes. That truth needs to be revealed through the way we live.

It is a wise witness to the world to reveal your love for God by raising up others and mobilizing people to think in the kind of true green thinking suggested in this book. Remind your friends and family members to take creation care seriously as part of their worship of the Creator who made them and redeemed them for something more.

My daughter-in-law inspired me in this regard. Standing outside a grocery store, we noticed a man sitting in his car, catching our attention because he dropped some paper trash out his window. She walked over gracefully, picked it up, and commented, "I'm sorry, sir, but I noticed this paper fall out of your car, is this something you need?   Or would you like me to carry it over to the trash can for you?" Her gentle tone disarmed any wrong attitude or threat that may have been perceived. Her warm mannerism was amazingly educational and redemptive. She lovingly revealed her concern for God's creation.

Speaking of the idea of revealing, there is a fascinating verse in the last book of the Bible, the book of Revelation:

> The fifth angel sounded his trumpet, and I saw a star that had fallen from the sky to the earth. The star was given the key to the shaft of the Abyss. When he opened the Abyss, smoke rose from it like the smoke from a gigantic furnace. The sun and sky were darkened by the smoke from the Abyss. And out of the smoke locusts came down upon the earth and were given power like that of scorpions of the earth. They were told not to harm the grass of the earth or any plant or tree, but only those people who did not have the seal of God on their foreheads (Rev. 9:1-4).

I find it interesting that the locusts which came down upon the earth were told not to harm the grass or any plant or tree. However you interpret images like this in the book of Revelation, there is something revealing about an instruction to destructive creatures not to harm the greens of the earth.

It is honorable to engage every opportunity to reveal your love for God's creation and your interest to participate in creation care. General revelation reveals the existence and the presence of God. Join the forces tasked to reveal Him.

Resource

I enjoyed doing a painting on my day off one week. Oil painting has become a therapeutic way to enter into a creative world of soul rest and refreshment. It's not a great skill for me, but a hobby I enjoy. In some ways it connects me with both art and science, creativity in creation.

Leonardo da Vinci (1452-1519) was best known as a masterful painter. His famous painting, The Last Supper, shows insights into his heart with the creation of a picture that has stirred the souls of multitudes of people, bearing witness of his faith.

Leonardo da Vinci has also been considered by many to be the real founder of modern science. He was an experimental scientist long before the development of the "scientific method." His scientific notebooks are filled with studies and notes about problems in anatomy, physics, biology, and even aeronautics. These have become resources that have been shared to inspire others.

Resources abound for helping people embrace the idea of creation care. There is evidence in creation of built-in mechanisms for creation control, examples of God holding it all together. Black-headed gulls, for example, have been known to save forests in Utah and Scotland by eating caterpillars that had infested forests. If creatures can be God's instrument to protect creation and hold things together, how much more effective can your hands be.

It is wise to resource other people in this regard. Share in what you have learned. Be contagious as you reflect on the beauty of God in creation. Reduce your use of resources as a good steward. Reuse and recycle as an act of worship. Reveal to others your appreciation for God as the Creator, and resource your friends with what you are doing and the lessons you are learning that help you to grow and become more *green*.

Living Water is Greener

After living in climates that were dry to semi-arid deserts, I came to really appreciate water. Although we take for granted the privilege of drinkable water coming right out of the tap, to live beyond green is to conserve and to say thanks for God's provision.

As a hunter and hiker, I have grown to love the feel of cool water in a fresh mountain stream, free flowing and abundant. There is nothing quite like a cool drink of refreshing water when thirsty.

There is also a thirst in the depths of the heart for the living God. We thirst to worship something. We have deep within us an emptiness that longs to be filled, a dryness that needs refreshment, a longing that needs to be satisfied.

Jesus used this crucial natural resource, water, to speak profound spiritual truth. At a well one day, He spoke to a woman and said, "Everyone who drinks of this water will thirst again; but whoever drinks of the water that I will give him shall never thirst; but the water that I will give him will become in him a well of water springing up to eternal life" (John 4:13-14). Jesus was speaking of pure, clean, abundant, refreshing, real water. Living water satisfies the longings of the heart, and this is water found only through a relationship with Him. He is the Creator of water and the source of genuine supply for the thirsty soul.

We spent some time at the source of Spring Creek one morning, a beautiful stream which serves as the source of drinking water for Lewistown, Montana. It is known as some of the purest water in the world. The source springs are a very peaceful and refreshing place.

The bubbling waters opened the tap of a wonderful discussion as we sat in admiration of God's source of water to life downstream. It reminded me of the references in Jeremiah 2:13 and 17:13, where God is referred to as the spring of living water.

I don't understand all the geology, but I do know that watching the bubbles at the springs inspired curiosity. Something significant was happening beneath the surface. The Christian life is like that. Much happens beneath the surface, deep in the heart, as we spend time in Bible Study and prayer. From that source spring of the deeper life there is an overflow, bubbling forth from a peaceful place unto the regions beyond. I would love to imagine people getting curious about the bubbling peace seen in Christ followers. The

Christian has living water as their source of hope, joy, and tranquility.

There is a wonderful mystery involved in observing water like that in Spring Creek. Looking at the peaceful springs at the source, it seems to defy logic when you stand downstream to observe so much water flowing so fast and so full. The amount of water flowing to the places beyond doesn't seem to match the quiet bubbling place of it's source. What happens beneath the surface is more significant than we might ever imagine. What happens when we spend time in prayer and worship unto God is much deeper than we might ever dream. Acts of creation care might have more of an overflowing influence than you would ever envision.

Spring Creek is known for its pure water, its beauty, and for providing a wonderful environment for fish and other wildlife. Many people discover the joy and fun of tubing, swimming, and fishing this wonderful Lewistown stream. The people of the area would affirm that the world is a better place because of that particular river. The world is also a better place because of you. Let if flow.

Close But Far

A man was reported missing in the Wind River Mountains of Wyoming. After several weeks, he was found near a secluded lake. He had failed to survive the elements. The scenario indicated that he had been walking across a rock field bordering the lake, and a shifting boulder caused him to fall and trap his leg. After many hours, he probably became dehydrated and terribly thirsty. He had tied strings together and attached them to his water bottle, attempting to throw it to the lake to get some water in his final hours. The bottle landed very close to the water, but not close enough. One more link on his string might have made the difference. He died in sight of and very near to the life-saving waters along his path.

That would be a painful end, being so close and yet so far. It seems a good way to remember and honor that man by considering an important message about God. He is above and beyond, wanting to lead us to still waters of peace. Consider this passage from the Bible:

He split the rocks in the desert and gave them water as abundant as the seas; he brought streams out of a rocky crag and made water flow down like rivers. But they continued to sin against him, rebelling in the desert against the Most High. They willfully put God to the test by demanding the food they craved. They spoke against God, saying, 'Can God spread a table in the desert? When he struck the rock, water gushed out, and streams flowed abundantly. But can he also give us food? Can he supply meat for his people?' (Psalm 78:15-20)

The questions are rhetorical. God can and God does provide. The greatest provision is Himself. Jesus Christ is the living water that brings refreshment to the thirsty soul and salvation to the dying heart. We all know of people who seem close to Christ and yet they are so far away. Perhaps their theology is off, perhaps they are reaching in the wrong direction, perhaps they are stuck in bolder fields of their own making. Perhaps you have been there. Perhaps you are there today. Pray that God will enable you to reach out and dip into His living waters.

He is within reach. He is worth reaching for and worthy of your worship. You can know personally and intimately the One who said, "If you knew the gift of God and who it is that asks you for a drink, you would have asked him and he would have given you living water" (John 4:10). He also said, "Whoever believes in me, as the Scripture has said, streams of living water will flow from within him (John 7:38-39). Or, as the writer of the final Bible book said, "For the Lamb at the center of the throne will be their shepherd; he will lead them to springs of living water. "And God will wipe away every tear from their eyes" (Rev. 7:17). Walking beyond green is walking with Jesus, the source of life.

Water is to be shared. Everyone needs water, and everyone needs to worship. While having lunch together, a friend began to take a drink of ice water and accidentally dropped his glass. The glass shattered when it hit the table. Water went everywhere, including into the lap of his girlfriend next to him. He hid his embarrassment well and was able to laugh, revealing much about his joyful character balanced with mature concern. Seizing the moment, we had a great discussion about living water and how it is not designed to be held within the confines of a glass.

Water is meant to be contained only in a temporary way for the purpose of taking it in. It is not to be poured into a jar and set on a shelf. Have you ever had a drink of the water you left sitting on your nightstand from the night before? Water needs to flow in order to stay fresh, moving to places in need of its life giving qualities. It is for distribution, not containment. It is to nourish you and to be shared, not held back and restrained. This is demonstrated all throughout creation. Would you rather drink from a stagnant green pond or a flowing mountain stream?

Water is to be appreciated, enjoyed, and given to others. Conserving is therefore about others. Taking care of our water supplies is about joining God in insuring that water arrives where it is needed. As the psalmist wrote, "He opened the rock and water flowed out; It ran in the dry places like a river" (Psalm 105:41). Words like that prompt worship.

You've heard the old saying that the grass is always greener on the other side of the fence. Perhaps the fence is not the issue. It is not about the barriers or obstacles. Perhaps the grass is greener where it is cared for and watered. Wherever you are, have some water with you, living water sourced by prayer. That opens a stream to experience greener pastures beyond. That is a great way to go a step past where people expect you to end up.

I hope for more contagious Christians to step forward in creation stewardship. We need to share the pure refreshment of life sustained by life giving waters of God's provision. Opportunities abound to make the world a better place through a life beyond green.

He will make your righteousness shine like the dawn,
the justice of your cause like the noonday sun.
~Psalm 37:6

The path of the righteous is like the first gleam of dawn,
shining ever brighter till the full light of day.
~Prov. 4:18~

For Reflection/Discussion:

1. Discuss the above verses.
2. Tell your story. How has Jesus held your life together, or how would you like Him to?
3. Spend some time out in nature and reflect.
4. What is your practice of recycling, reducing, or reusing? Give yourself a challenge.
5. Who in your world might God desire you to resource so that they can capture a deeper concern for creation?
6. Who in your world needs a fresh drink? Pray for them.
7. Would you like a creative challenge? Spend some time under a tree and write a prayer, song, or poem that expresses your gratitude for the God of Creation.

A Sunset Love Affair, By Greg Asimakoupoulos

Lord, Your creation causes me
To open my mouth and say "awe!"
Before rolling over and falling asleep
The sun kissed the watching clouds
Causing them to blush.
And in the hush that followed
You reached down and caressed me.
And I raised my hands
And lifted my voice
In praise of the fact
That I am loved.[56]

~APPENDIX~

Ideas for Creation Care

1. Print on both sides of paper to reduce the amount of paper you use.
2. Make recycling more convenient....place paper, plastic, can, and glass bins in convenient locations, especially after gathering events.
3. Purchase or make composting bins to reduce trash.
4. Instead of using water in plastic bottles, use reusable bottles with your logo on them.
5. Use reusable or biodegradable plates, bowls, and utensils for meal events.
6. Post reminder signs that encourage turning off lights and turning down thermostats in rooms not in use, including creative Bible verses.
7. Adjust and monitor thermostats---set to 68 in fall and winter (instead of 72) and 74 (instead of 68) in warmer months.
8. Give computers a rest by setting them to hibernate after 30 minutes of inactivity and monitors to sleep after 5-20 minutes.
9. Use power strips to shut down equipment.
10. Replace traditional bulbs with compact fluorescent ones which can use up to 75% less energy.
11. Encourage carpooling and alternative modes of transportation like biking and walking.
12. Focus on and give to ministries that are "Green." (ecologically conscious) and champion their initiative.
13. Gather a group of Christians to do a "Green confession booth" and apologize to people for the lack of creation concern exhibited by the church.
14. Teach love for animals and creation.
15. Appoint a task force to do a "green audit" of your church or organization, using utility companies and private contractors to look for ways to save on energy use and office processes.
16. Offer the opportunity for recycling at your facility.

17. Teach gardening. Form gardening groups or clubs who study the Bible together and enjoy creation care.
18. Set up a recycle shop at your church, business, or facility.
19. Encourage people to buy green (recycled paper, printer ink that uses vegetable oil, etc.).
20. Encourage green prayer (see chapter 9).
21. Mobilize teams of people to pick up trash in an urban neighborhood.
22. Include the idea of "less is more" in your teaching on stewardship. Using less of everything, including electricity, water, gas, paper printer ink, etc., leaves more for others and does more for creation care.
23. Expand your teaching of Christian stewardship to include taking care of creation and the resources God provides.
24. Encourage people to place old and unused bulletins and publications in the recycle bin rather than throwing them away.
25. Take nature walks to help appreciate the creation of the Creator.
26. Build a prayer garden or prayer walk that includes displays with Bible verses that celebrate the God of creation.
27. Go paperless where possible.
28. Teach children about creation care and sustainable living.
29. Hold contests for poems and songs written about declaring God's glory in creation.
30. Display posters and pictures that declare the glory of God in His beautiful creation.
31. Plant a tree....or two or three.
32. File and reuse song sheets and other copied materials.
33. Adopt a highway.
34. Come up with some creative marques on your sign:
    - *God turns trash into treasure---recycle*
    - *The God of creation involves us in recreation*
    - *Don't destroy nature, enjoy it*
    - *Recreation includes Re-creation*
    - *God created----be a steward*
    - *Save water---water saves*

35. Include in your publications ideas of how to reuse and recycle resources.
36. Fuel some dreams with people to be innovative in the world of biomimicry.
37. Host a craft show that puts on display how one persons "junk" can become another persons useful treasure, highlighting the making of beautiful things from things discarded.
38. Join the ranks of parents switching to cloth diapers.
39. Do a study on the trees mentioned in Isaiah 55:13.
40. Use water filters rather than bottled water.
41. Wash and reuse Ziploc bags rather than trashing them.

Reaching Beyond Green

Like a tree
I want to reach higher
   I want more to be
      To God's glory in me
         a beyond green fire.
Yet a tension unfurls
Somewhere between roots and sky
Torn between two worlds
Rooted in soil ◄──► reaching on high

It seems more real
To grip in fingers the earth
Soil we can see and feel
Hands can hold the dirt

Leaves can't quite grasp
Unable to hold the sky
But the essence of the air
Enters pores alive.

The Sun keeps cells moving
Sunshine enters the core of life
What the earth can't fully bring
Light inspires a reach that is right.

Lord, help my outstretched arms
To never be pulled back
Compromising searches only harm
Sending roots where true nutrients lack.

Help me not to burrow deeper
To simple things I feel and see and cling
But reaching higher for you my Keeper
True risen life you bring.[57]

Ideas for Worshiping God in Creation

1. Watch a sunset and read a psalm aloud, to God and anyone else with you.
2. Sit quietly in the forest and watch for how many insects and animals you can detect, keeping yourself unseen and your Bible open.
3. The next time you see a colorful sunset, clap your hands in appreciation for God and thank Him.
4. Tell God how creative He is the next time you see an intriguing insect, a colorful plant, a majestic mountain, a pristine lake, or a beautiful animal.
5. Write a song or poem while sitting in the shade of a sugar maple tree in the fall.
6. Take a walk in the rain and smile with gratitude for the moisture and all that it means.
7. Listen to the songs of a bird and try to imitate it with a whistle while thanking God in your heart.
8. Take some time to look at the clouds and thank God for the various shapes that remind you of Him and the people in your world.
9. Spend some time on a hillside and ask God to open your eyes to lessons He may want to teach you through His creation around you.
10. Stop to smell the roses, but thank God when you do.
11. Walk along a beach and thank God for the waves of mercy and grace that continue to come out of the ocean of his love.
12. When God opens your eyes to creation lessons, share your thoughts with other people.
13. When you meet people who care about creation, pray with and for them, with gratitude.
14. Read Isaiah 40:26 on a clear night and have a time of thankful prayer as you consider the stars.

Discovering a Restored Relationship With God

Origins in the garden of Eden were wonderful. The open love relationship with the God of the universe was the best of it----- Unhindered, unimaginable, intimate, honest love. Read about it in the first two chapters of Genesis.

Then came the storm. A wrong choice was made by the first humans. That choice, influenced by deception, opened the door to the hurricane of what we call the fall. What happened was a severed relationship characteristic of the world each person is now born into, a broken world. God's desire is to restore a relationship with Him, repair relationships with others, and involve us in the ministry of reconciliation and restoration of the world.

To find the path to life, you must first realize where you are:

The first question God asked is found in Genesis 3:9, "Where are you?" It's not like God didn't know where they were. The question was pointed, giving an opportunity for Adam and Eve to be honest, vulnerable, and repentant.

Every person is born separated from God, in a state of sin, emptiness, and death. ALL have sinned (Romans 3:23) because we were born in a world of sin and separation from God (Romans 5:12).

God, our Creator, wants us to experience life in an intimate love relationship with Him. However, there is a problem. Heaven's standard is perfection; there will be NO SIN in heaven. That is one reason that heaven will be so great. The main reason, however, is that God is there. He loves us, but because of His justice He must do something about our sin.

So, be honest, where are you?

Because of our sin, there is a grand canyon between us and God, a wall of separation.

Consider this verse in the Bible and the diagram that visualizes it:

"For the wages of sin is death, but the free gift of God is eternal life through Christ Jesus our Lord" (Romans 6:23).

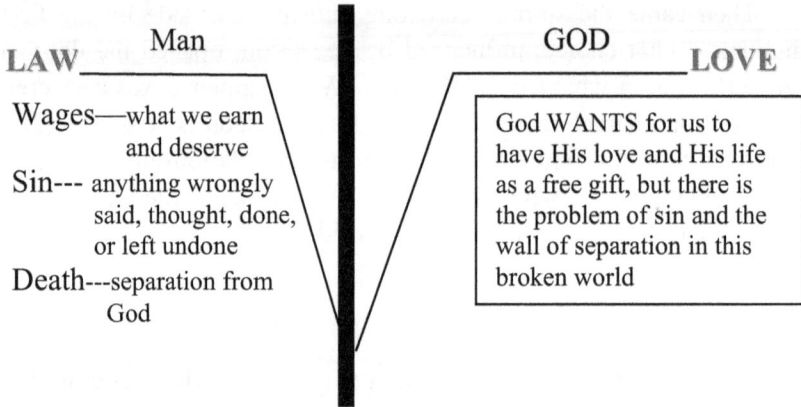

LAW _____ Man   GOD _____ LOVE

Wages—what we earn and deserve
Sin--- anything wrongly said, thought, done, or left undone
Death---separation from God

God WANTS for us to have His love and His life as a free gift, but there is the problem of sin and the wall of separation in this broken world

No attempts of man can bridge the gap or penetrate the wall, so God did for us what we could never do ourselves. While we were still sinners, Christ died for us (Romans 5:8). He took our place. He paid the penalty for sin. His death on the cross formed the bridge to heaven. Jesus said "I am the way, the truth, and the life, no man comes to the Father except through me" (John 14:6).

THERE IS A SOLUTION!

If we confess with our mouth that Jesus is Lord, and believe in our heart that God raised Him from the dead, we will be saved.
(Romans 10:9)

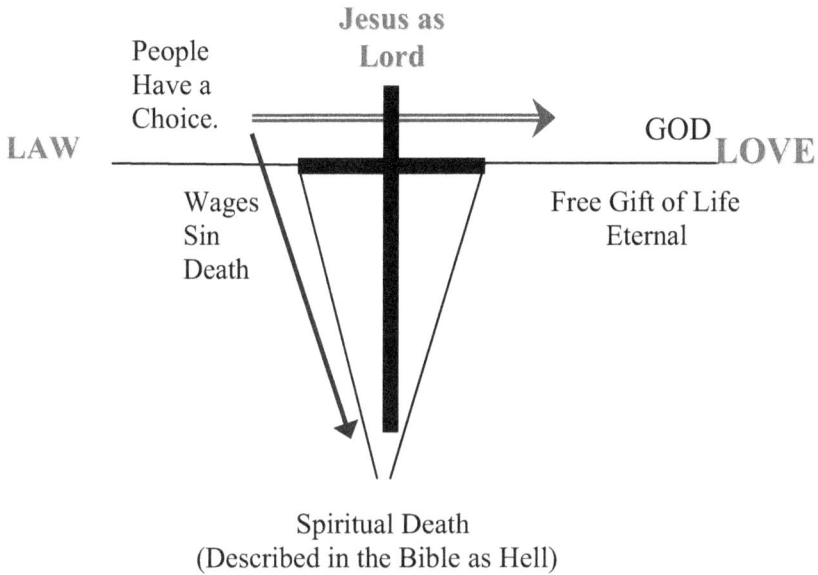

Spiritual Death
(Described in the Bible as Hell)

Jesus took our place. We call it a substitutionary sacrifice. He died for our sins. The horror of the cross shows us how bad sin is, but it also displays the depth of His love. At the cross, with outstretched arms, He declares, "I love you this much." We each have a choice: Reject God and have the consequences of that decision forever, or receive salvation and abundant life in Christ. When we respond by receiving Jesus as Lord and Savior, we cross over from death (forever without God) to LIFE (forever with God)! That isn't just about a future in heaven, it means abundant life now.

Jesus said, "I have come that they may have life, and have it to the full" (John 10:10b). He also said, "I tell you the truth, whoever hears my word and believes him who sent me has eternal life and will not be condemned; he has crossed over from death to life" (John 5:24-25).

You can cross over from death to life.

**Whoever calls upon the name of the Lord
will be saved!** (Romans 10:13)

Talk to God, say a prayer, call upon Him. He is very near.

ACKNOWLEDGE to God that you are lost. Admit that you have sinned, that you are far from perfect. You may not be as bad as some people, but the standard God calls for is perfection (Matt. 5:48). There is no hope for you to be perfected without the perfection of Jesus Christ in your life. Acknowledge that you need Him. Confess to God that you have blown it, that you are what the Bible calls a sinner. Acknowledge your need to repent, to change your mind and your direction. Ask for His help.

BELIEVE that Jesus died for your sins at the cross; He took your place. He paid the penalty for your sin. Believe that He rose from the dead to give you life. The resurrection is very real and the power of the resurrection is for you to realize and live.

Confess with your mouth that Jesus is Lord. Give thanks as you receive the free gift of eternal life. Ask Jesus into your heart as both LORD and SAVIOR. Trust Him as your Lord and Leader to guide you into the abundance of life eternal. Follow Jesus and get involved in a local church, a community of faith that teaches the Bible. Embrace Christ and engage His mission.

**"I tell you the truth, whoever hears my word and believes him who
sent me has eternal life and will not be condemned; he has crossed
over from death to life"** (John 5:24)

And that is a promise!

About the Author

Steve has had a broad exposure to God's creation. Hunting, fishing, camping, and outdoor activities were a form of religion for him earlier in life. Then He had an encounter with the God of Creation which transformed his life. He and Kristi discovered the wonderful abundant life of following Jesus, and have grown in their love for the outdoors in much deeper ways as a result.

Steve has worked in camping ministries, the logging industry, wildlife research, ranching, firefighting, and factory work. He served as a soldier in the United States Marine Corps and has also been a security guard, furniture delivery man, teacher, special education aid, administrator, missionary teacher overseas, pastor, dorm parent, adjunct faculty at a Bible college, and a church planter. His passion for creation stewardship as an act of worship and honor to the Creator fueled his completion of this book.

Steve is available to speak at outdoor functions, hunter banquets, or wild game feasts. You can contact Steve or Kristi and order bulk copies of this book through their family website, www.thediehls.net.

Index of Bible Verses

Hosea
14:8-9......29

Jonah
4............61

Habakkuk
2:20.........59

Zechariah
2:13........43

Matthew
1:20.........49
4:17.........65
5:14-16.....57
6:9-13...53, 65,133
6:19-21.....90
6:25-30......68, 129
8:23-27......70
13:23.........97
16:24-26....95, 103
17:20-21.....51
22:39.........10
25:14-30....21,22
28:3-4.......52

Mark
4:41.........28
6:39.........7
8:34.........93
10:45........21
11............62

Luke
1:31.........49
4:42.........38
9:23.........96
10:9-11......65
11:45.........12
13:18-19.....59
14:27.........98
19:10.........70
19:41.........12
20:38........103

John
1:3-4......70
3:16-17....11, 69
4:10-14...12,146,
          140, 144
7:38-39....12, 146
8:58.........46
9:6-7.........11
9:36.........140
10:1-18...37, 38, 140
13:34-35......13
14:6-7.........12, 38
15:5-8.......71, 109
20:26.........37
21.............39

Acts
4:24.........132
5:21.........39
10:19-23......109
9:1-22.........50
17:28.........78

Romans
1:20......26, 40, 54,
          58, 76, 104
6:11.........97
8:19-23.........64
8:28-29........132

1 Corinthians
1:18.........106
2:7.............46
4:1-2.........76
10:31.........53
15:31.........96
16:13-14.......25

2 Corinthians
3:18.........57
4:5.............55
5:17............103
10:7ff..........136

Galatians
5:22-24.........72
6:2.............14
6:15.........96

Ephesians
2:10..........2, 90
6:14..........136

Philippians
1:21.........97
2:6-11....21, 66
2:14-16......38, 55
3:7-14.......99, 117

Colossians
1:16-17.......135
3:5.............95
3:17...........53

1 Thessalonians
5:16-18......37

1 Timothy
4:8...........78

2 Timothy
1:7............65

Titus
2:11-14.......131

Hebrews
4:12...........26
11:1..........136
12:2...........49

1 Peter
2:5.............137
5:12..........137

1 John
4:7-16.......14, 16

Revelation
1:14-15.........53
4:8.............45
7:17.............146
9:1-4......142
11:18.......66
22:5.....56
21:23....57
21-22.......73-74

NOTES

Chapter One

[1] Shane Riggs, *Harnessing the Wind, the Water, and the Sun; An Oldtown Couple's Eco Friendly Mountain Dreamhouse* (Allegany Magazine, Volume 5, Issue Two, April/May 2010), 50. The author reports, "The home they built contains solar panels for geo thermal electricity, a private windmill that stores and generates electricity by harnessing winds from 10 to 75 mph and an alternative wood burning furnace for heat that leaves a neutral carbon footprint."

[2] David Powlison, *A Praying Life* (NavPress, 2009), 20.

Chapter Two

[3] Tony Campolo, *How to Rescue the Earth Without Worshiping Nature* (Thomas Nelson Publishers, Nashville 1992), 199.

[4] Institute in Basic Youth Conflicts, Inc., *Character Sketches, Volume I* (1976 Institute in Basic Youth Conflicts, Inc), 210.

[5] David W. Henderson, *This is My Father's World* (Discipleship Journal, Issue Eighty-One, 1994), 19.

[6] David W. Henderson, *This is My Father's World* (Discipleship Journal, Issue Eighty-One, 1994), 19.

Chapter Three

[7] 1 Tim. 4:16, 2 Tim. 4:3, Titus 1:9 and Titus 2:1 are among the Scriptures that instruct us to be very careful what we teach and to guard our doctrine closely.

[8] "For since the creation of the world God's invisible qualities---his eternal power and divine nature---have been clearly seen, being understood from what has been made, so that men are without excuse."

[9] Robert E. Webber, *Ancient-Future Worship; Proclaiming and Enacting God's Narrative* (Baker Books, 2008), 40.

[10] SCUBA = self-contained underwater breathing apparatus.

Chapter Four

[11] Trevor Persaud, *Christ of the Klingons* (Christianity Today, December 2010), 47.

[12] Fred Heeren, *The Message from Space* (New Man magazine, July/August 1995), 34.

[13] Fred Heeren, *The Message from Space* (New Man magazine, July/August 1995), 34.

[14] Jesse Jorgensen, in a personal email dated October 31, 2012.

[15] Henry Morris, *Men of Science Men of God* (Master Book Pbl., 1984), 34.

[16] David W. Henderson, *This is My Father's World* (Discipleship Journal Issue Eighty-One, 1994), 20.

Chapter Five
[17] Institute in Basic Youth Conflicts, Inc., *Character Sketches, Volume I* (1976 Institute in Basic Youth Conflicts, Inc), 35.
[18] Institute in Basic Youth Conflicts, Inc., *Character Sketches, Volume I* (1976 Institute in Basic Youth Conflicts, Inc), 269.
[19] Tony Campolo, *How to Rescue the Earth Without Worshiping Nature* (Thomas Nelson Publishers, Nashville 1992), 127.
[20] Calvin B. DeWitt, *Myth 2; It's Not Biblical to Be Green* (Christianity Today, April 4, 1994), 30.
[21] Tony Campolo, *How to Rescue the Earth Without Worshiping Nature* (Thomas Nelson Publishers, Nashville 1992), 88-89.
[22] Dr. Jim Lindsey, in an email dated 10/23/2012.
[23] Robert E. Webber, *Ancient-Future Worship; Proclaiming and Enacting God's Narrative* (Baker Books, 2008), 59.
[24] Matt Redman, *Heart of Worship* (Hillsong)
[25] http://www.parrotmountainandgardens.com/

Chapter Six
[26] Pastor Ernie Lambright, in an email dated 10/23/2012
[27] Henry Morris, *Men of Science Men of God* (Master Book Pbl., 1984), 46.
[28] Anne Morrow Lindbergh, *Gift from the Sea* (Pantheon Books, New York, 1983), 17.
[29] John Ray, *The Wisdom of God Manifested in the Works of the Creation* (London, 1717, Nabu Public Domain, Reprint), 25.
[30] David Nowak, USDA Forest Service Study
[31] Roger S. Ulrich, Science Magazine
[32] David N. Livingstone, *Myth 1; The Church is To Blame* (Christianity Today, April 4, 1994), 24.

Chapter Seven
[33] Dietrich Bonhoeffer, *The Cost of Discipleship* (Touchstone, 1995).
[34] A. B. Simpson, *Days of Heaven on Earth* (Christian Publications, 1984) November 23rd.
[35] Robert E. Webber, *Ancient-Future Worship; Proclaiming and Enacting God's Narrative* (Baker Books, 2008), 33.
[36] Fred Heeren, *The Message from Space* (New Man magazine, July/August 1995), 30.
[37] Robert E. Webber, *Ancient-Future Worship; Proclaiming and Enacting God's Narrative* (Baker Books, 2008), 34.
[38] Robert E. Webber, *Ancient-Future Worship; Proclaiming and Enacting God's Narrative* (Baker Books, 2008), 35.
[39] Robert E. Webber, *Ancient-Future Worship; Proclaiming and Enacting God's Narrative* (Baker Books, 2008), 37.

Chapter Eight
[40] A distinction is evident in Genesis 2:20 between wild animals and livestock. Livestock includes animals raised for food. If animals can be raised for food, it must be ok to harvest wild game for food.

---

[41] Todd Tanner, *Why I Hunt* (Montana Outdoors, November-December 2012), 25.

[42] Steve Chapman, *A Hunter Sets His Sights; Taking Aim at What Really Matters in Life* (Harvest House Publishers, 2000), 7.

Chapter Nine

[43]Tony Campolo, *How to Rescue the Earth Without Worshiping Nature* (Thomas Nelson Publishers, Nashville 1992), 116.

[44] L.B. Cowman, *Streams in the Desert* (Zondervan 1997), July 8th entry 264.

[45] Paul introduced himself in many of his epistles as a "servant" or a "slave" of Christ. He wrote to the Corinthian church, "For he who was a slave when he was called by the Lord is the Lord's freedman; similarly, he who was a free man when he was called is Christ's slave" (1 Cor. 7:22-23).

[46] Janine Benyus, *The Promise of Biomimicry* (TED Talk, 2012, http://www.ted.com/talks/janine_benyus_shares_nature_s_designs.html)

[47] http://www.mnn.com/earth-matters. The scientists involved in this research and design suggest that if cargo ships can squeeze out even a single percent in efficiency using this technology, they burn less bunker oil and don't require cleaning chemicals for their hulls.   Scientists are applying the technique to create surfaces in hospitals that resist bacteria growth.

[48] http://www.mnn.com/earth-matters. This website gives great examples of how innovation has been inspired by designs found in nature.

[49] http://www.mnn.com/earth-matters. Professor Ilan Kroo leads this team of researchers at Stanford University.

[50] http://www.asknature.org

[51] John Ray, *The Wisdom of God Manifested in the Works of the Creation* (London, 1717, Nabu Public Domain, Reprint), 88.

[52] Robert E. Webber, *Ancient-Future Worship; Proclaiming and Enacting God's Narrative* (Baker Books, 2008), 170.

Chapter Ten

[53] David W. Henderson, *This is My Father's World* (Discipleship Journal, Issue Eighty-One, 1994), 20.

[54] Anne Morrow Lindbergh, *Gift from the Sea* (Pantheon Books, New York, 1983), 54-55.

[55] Loren Wilkinson, *Myth 3; There is Nothing Christians Can Do* (Christianty Today, April 4, 1994), 32.

[56] Greg Asimakoupoulos, *Prayers from my Pencil* (Mainstay Church Resources, 2001) 22.

Appendix:

[57] Inspired by the writing of Ken Gire, *Windows of the Soul* (Zondervan 1996), 49.

www.ingramcontent.com/pod-product-compliance
Lightning Source LLC
Chambersburg PA
CBHW020002290326
41935CB00007B/276